I Am: The Way, Truth & Life

Ernest Curry

WESTBOW
PRESS®
A DIVISION OF THOMAS NELSON
& ZONDERVAN

WestBow Press books may be ordered through booksellers or by contacting:

WestBow Press
A Division of Thomas Nelson & Zondervan
1663 Liberty Drive
Bloomington, IN 47403
www.westbowpress.com
1 (866) 928-1240

ISBN: 978-1-5127-9838-8 (sc)
ISBN: 978-1-5127-9839-5 (hc)
ISBN: 978-1-5127-9837-1 (e)

Library of Congress Control Number: 2017912006

Printed in USA

WestBow Press rev. date: 10/02/2017

It all started with Him, the Alpha and Omega. Thank You, Lord, for this journey and blessing. I dedicate this to You.

ACKNOWLEDGMENTS

Many thanks to my family for standing by me during this journey with my Lord and Savior. I also wish to express appreciation for my wife's dedication and influence, my mother's guidance and wisdom, my dad's mentorship and steadfastness, and the creativity and knowledge of my sisters, Brooke and Morgan. To my sons, may you grow into faithful men of God and influence many for the kingdom.

PREFACE

Our path to the Father is through Jesus, and Jesus directs us to Him. When I think about God and how He speaks to us, I am reminded of a light wind on a summer's day. The wind is almost needed at that exact time to keep us cool. It provides comfort in our worst moments. Just when we need God in certain instances, He provides love.

My Creator expressed the need to write this book, and I feel that what is important to Him must be shared. My prayer for this book is that it will find you well. The Father uses my pen to express the design He has for this, and I am grateful. As I gather my thoughts and prepare my mind to speak as a facilitator for the Lord, natural questions come to my mind. Why would the Creator of all things love us? Why does He show such compassion to this world, a place of evil and sin? Yes, it is our nature to sin; that is true. Why would the Creator develop us to have the choice to sin against His kingdom?

Jesus said, "If ye had known me, ye should have known my Father also: and from henceforth ye know him, and have seen him" (John 14:7). Jesus spoke and in this portrayed "I AM." For if you have truly known Jesus, you know the Father—but not only know the Father. You have experienced Him, because you have seen "I AM" through Jesus. I have the feeling in society that it is so easy to take this truth for granted. A man in true form was born to a virgin; He was and still is God and was sacrificed perfectly for our sins. Only through His death can a world that would disobey and proclaim His nonexistence have a path to Him, a path of salvation.

"Then spake Jesus again unto them, saying, I am the light of the world: he that followeth me shall not walk in darkness, but shall have the light of life" (John 8:12). He not only loves us but also *unconditionally* loves us. Every single sin committed ran through Jesus on the day He died.

I remember the story of a man who died and met the Lord, and I would like to share it to set the stage for this book. An older man died and went to heaven during his emergency surgery. During his visit with God, "I AM" asked the man whether he had any questions before his return to earth. The man thought and thought. I mean, if you could ask God one question, what would it be? The man didn't know what to ask and then he chuckled.

God said, "What is it that is so funny?"

The man replied, "God, what is the meaning of life?"

God laughed a bit and said, "It is really simple. Love."

Love in itself is unquestionable but unanswerable. It is the one thing that is indefinite and intangible in our lives. To take it one step further, it still exists. Many things come and go, but love will last forever. Simply put, God is love.

"You are my witness," declares the Lord, "and my servant whom I have Chosen that you may know and believe me and understand that I am He. Before Me no god was formed, not shall there be any after."

(Isa. 43:10 ESV)

"I am the Lord, your Holy One, the Creator of Israel, your King."

(Isa. 43:15 ESV)

DAY 1

Lifestyle

"For whether we live, we live unto the Lord; and whether we die, we die unto the Lord: whether we live therefore, or die, we are the Lord's" (Rom. 14:8). Living for Jesus isn't a task or lifestyle that comes easily. Jesus, formed with amazing grace and wisdom, lived perfectly as the Son of Man. Since the garden of Eden, we have been born into a sinful nature. We desire to sin, and we must recognize the difference between us and our Lord. Our journey on this earth is intended to prepare us for a life that is everlasting. Like a roller coaster, from start to finish, there will be a lot of unexpected twists.

We must continue to drive forward in our daily walk to ensure we see the end. We receive what we expect from our Father: our time, renewal, and compassionate faith. Time dedicated to the Father is time well received, for if we give nothing, we should expect nothing. If we come to Him, expecting growth, we will receive growth.

Over complication of the Father is a constant in this world, and we must strive to keep from placing earthly limitations on heavenly actions. The secret is that our Father is simple in nature. He has provided us with guidance through the Bible and direction through the Holy Spirit. Everything you see is a reminder of Him and His endless possibility. Yet we daily overlook this, busy in our little worlds, wants, and desires. A lifestyle for the Lord is living in His wants and desires for our lives, walking in His creation, and receiving His guidance for our decisions. Imagine the endless possibilities if we walk in His capability and follow His path designed for our feet.

Live with a mind-set of sacrifice like Paul and desire God's own heart like David did. Your true potential and the possibilities for success in Christ will be endless. We are here to facilitate for the kingdom; we must live in a manner so our actions portray Jesus.

In His hand is the life of every living thing and
breath of all mankind.

(Job 12:10 ESV)

DAY 2

Seasons

"He appointed the moon for seasons: the sun knoweth his going
down" (Ps. 104:19). As seasons come and go, we know what time
of year or season it is since there is a change in the environment.
God marks the seasons of life according to the differences in us or
the changes in our lives. Often we are blessed with the gifts of the
Spirit; during these times, we achieve what God has in store for
us. He uses seasons to guide our walk and bring us closer to Him.

Seasons are a time for learning what God has in mind for
us and how we are to be used for eternal service to others. He
speaks to us in many ways; like a tug on the heart, His words
can be missed if we aren't listening. Trust in the Lord with a
childlike mentality. When He talks, listen; where He directs, go.
An unheard message can be life and death. We understand that
He is life, which is the answer to the test we are looking for. He
wants to use us in many indescribable ways. Some may not even
make sense, but we must be able to take God out of the box we so
often place Him in. We should broaden our image of Him and let
His ideas flood our imaginations.

God in nature is unconventional, and in earthly understanding
He is all and very similar to matter we all learned about in science
class. Everything is matter in some way or another; and like
matter, He exists. He is all around us and in us. Think of Him
like air; you can't see it, but it is all around us, and we need it to
survive. Because of the perfect sacrifice (Jesus), we are now given
access to the Holy Father. Jesus, in His final season on earth

as a living, breathing man, took all our sins, and our sins were placed on Him for that day. Jesus carried our heavy hearts and our worst moments. At that time He was separated from God, His Father. For the first time, they were separated; this was His saddest moment. When Jesus passed, the curtain in the temple, used to separate man from God in the place of the most holy, was torn. This act represents our forgiveness; our sins were made clean. That was the day. We, the unworthy, could have a one-on-one relationship with the "I AM."

And that all this assembly may know that the Lord saves not with sword and spear. For the battle is the Lord's, and He will give you into our hand.

(1 Sam. 17:47 ESV)

DAY 3

Goliath

How can you measure what's unmeasurable? How can a metaphor stand between you and what God has in store for your life? Breaking through the chains of life may be the most challenging obstacle you face. God has so much in mind for us, but we spend most of our lives' opportune times trying to defeat our Goliaths.

God gave Goliath to David to show the world what a small shepherd boy was capable of. When he became a king, a man after God's heart, his military might couldn't be matched, but his blessings were from God. How much could God use us if we spent less time running from what God has planned for us and going after it with love and compassion to succeed for His kingdom? I challenge you today to stop the excuses of why or why not to complete what He has asked of you. Fulfill yourself with the Holy Spirit, and God will make a way for you. He will challenge you along the way to enable your spiritual growth.

God will continue to chase us and place Goliaths in our paths to ensure our success. He wants us to become part of His team to ensure the eternal destiny He has for our lives and how He can complete it. God knows how valuable we can be. By our efforts through the Father, we can be used as facilitators by witnessing to someone who could potentially be the next Billy Graham. He can equip us with the talent to bring crowds to Jesus. Many don't think they are talented and could ever do what Billy Graham has done. Sure, not everyone can speak in front of thousands of people or fill stadiums, but God knows someone who can, and through us, He makes a way.

I hate to speak publicly, but I know God will ask that of me. Again, He will give me a Goliath. That's how God trains us and teaches each of us every day. He gives us baby steps and smaller Goliaths. When ready, He will give us confidence in succeeding against larger Goliaths until we have fulfilled His blessings for us. The point isn't about the hardships. It's about succeeding in life for the kingdom of God.

"And now, O Lord God, the word that thou hast spoken concerning thy servant, and concerning his house, establish it forever, and do as thou hast said. And let thy name be magnified forever, saying, The Lord of hosts is the God over Israel: and let the house of thy servant David be established before thee" (2 Sam. 7:25–26).

When you pass through the waters, I will be with you; and through the rivers, they shall not overwhelm you; when you walk through fire you shall not be burned, and the flames shall not consume you.

(Isa. 43:2 ESV)

DAY 4

Battles

"And the Lord God said unto the serpent, because thou hast done this, thou art cursed above all cattle, and above every beast of the field; upon thy belly shalt thou go, and dust shalt thou eat all the days of thy life: And I will put enmity between thee and the woman, and between thy seed and her seed; it shall bruise thy head and thou shalt bruise his heel" (Gen. 3:14–15).

If we truly believe in Christ, we understand His death was the key to eternal life and to our determination to choose God and accept His light. Satan tempted Jesus in the wilderness, and the same is true with Eve. Satan chooses the time of his temptation and the grounds in which he sways us to his favor. He has to; without it the coward wouldn't be able to trick us in his game, which he so carefully plays. He takes our confidence and destroys it to the point of weakness and doubt. That is when he can act in our lives and use us to his benefit for his objectives in the world. It starts when we believe his lie and ends when we fall short of God's almighty glory.

You can choose to live for Satan or for God, but you cannot be lukewarm. Stay grounded in the Father and believe that in Him we are chosen for great and mighty things. God can use us for unimaginable feats. If we place His power inside our way of understanding, the abilities He can shower us with are constrained only by our imaginations. Limitations by default are placed where they aren't needed. Through our lack of faith, we are unable to achieve what miraculous goals He has set for us. Let me ask you this: why is Satan after you in the first place? Could it be that you are to be used for God's work? Or by your faith, could God use you to move mountains? Could it be that Satan knows you will assist in the fight for his demise? Satan is a weakling and a coward; he will steal, kill, and destroy. He knows the truth; he is already defeated. So, by default, he wants to take you and everyone around you with him. There is hope in Jesus. Our sins were placed on the cross with Jesus, and He defeated all Satan's lies and powers.

When your burdens become heavy and your battle becomes too much, God knows. He is there so you can place your heavy yoke at His feet. He will not only carry it for you but also take you to higher and more valuable places to use you for the kingdom of God. Jesus used His knowledge of the scripture, God's word, His free will to obey, and He overcame the battle against Satan in the wilderness. Satan is just a player in the game of light and darkness. The darkness is where he thrives; he cannot live with or around the light of the world. Be aware of his nature; beware of his lies and trickery. God has a plan for each of us. The proof is His death; His cross is our victory. Make your life worth His blood; that is the challenge.

But God shows His love for us in that while we were sinners, Christ died for us.

(Rom. 5:8 ESV)

DAY 5

God's Love

"For God so loved the world, that he gave his only begotten Son, that whosoever believeth in him should not perish, but have everlasting life. For God sent not his Son into the world to condemn the world; but that the world through him might be saved" (John 3:16–17). Knowing love is to know God, but not knowing love is to be without God. Sadly, something so simple is missed in our daily actions. Can we imagine that our portrayed actions, the ones that are without love, aren't with God and are what a nonbeliever could possibly take to the grave? I pray that my life will never be the one that interferes with God's work. God's love should make us question life in general. Nothing He has shown us is normal or conventional in action or terminology. Would you give up your child as a sacrifice for the world's sins? In your earthly shell, in your right mind, would you be physically able to place your child on a cross so a perfect sacrifice would cover the world's sin? Then why do so many people wonder, *If God is love?*

"And Jesus answered and said, Verily I say unto you, There is no man that hath left house, or brethren, or sisters, or father, or mother, or wife, or children, or lands, for my sake, and the gospel's, But he shall receive an hundredfold now in this time, houses, and brethren, and sisters, and mothers, and children, and lands, with persecutions; and in the world to come eternal life" (Mark 10:29–30). The disciples gave up so much to follow Christ, but are we any different? Have you felt the hardship of following God? Being a follower of Christ isn't easy, and in this

9

statement Jesus gives us confidence about our sacrifices for His kingdom. Love was born of a virgin as a man, putting an end to animal sacrifices; Jesus died as a perfect lamb, and He rose again, defeating the grave to give us power and knowledge.

By God's sacrifice, we can go into a world that disputes us and gives love back to free the enslaved. Satan binds the hearts of stone to hatred and death through opinions and actions. Free yourselves from this world; you can do so only with love. To know God's love is to have eternal life. To know bitterness is to be enslaved by the evils of the son of darkness.

For if you live according to the flesh you will die, but if by the spirit you put to death the deeds of body, you will live.

(Rom. 8:13 ESV)

DAY 6

Standard of Christ

Struggles, turmoil, and death in this world can take their toll. Every day we pay some kind of price physically and internally. We should be focused with sincere intentions to represent the Father's light through guidance and mentorship in our lives to the ones around us. I like to describe our daily walk as being similar to an archer looking for his or her bull's-eye. We shoot thousands of arrows, but only a few strike the bull's-eye. Over time and with practice, the archer gets better. His or her proficiency increases, and shooting the bull's-eye becomes more frequent.

Growing in Christ is very similar to being an archer. We are baptized, receiving light; and like the archer, we struggle to be in God's perfect image. But with sheer determination to succeed, we fire more shots over and over. Finally, we produce well-aimed, center-mass shots that strike our targets over and over. Our walk and growth have depth, and our passion to know our Father's love grows more rapidly. "That we henceforth be no more children, tossed to and fro, and carried about with every wind of doctrine, by the sleight of men, and cunning craftiness, whereby they lie in wait to deceive; But speaking the truth in love, may grow up into him in all things, which is the head, even Christ" (Eph. 4:14–15).

Live every day in the love of Christ, for that is God's light, which we strive to represent. Living in His light brings great joy to the Father, for He came as a living sacrifice for us. The Bible calls it a pleasant aroma for God that we give our all to live in love, for God is love, and we are to live in it. Life is made up of acts of living, and in living, our actions define us. What you do in this world defines you. Defining yourself in Christ and living in His standard bring a life that is open hearted for God's will. For achieving this, He will move through you, and your actions will be for His kingdom.

I cannot stress enough that the things of this earth that are worshipped daily aren't of the Father. Earthly nature isn't His nature, for we cannot fully grasp what His love and light entail, because they don't make earthly sense. The reason is simple. They aren't of this earth. Everything will come to pass; His light will expose the dark and the talks shared in silence. We cannot hide; thus, the reason we must live. Living to be in His light or be His mirror like image is the goal we strive for. "Knowing that whatsoever good thing any man doeth, the same shall he receive of the Lord, whether he be bond or free" (Eph. 6:8).

The fruit of the righteous is a tree of life, and whoever captures souls is wise.

(Prov. 11:30 ESV)

DAY 7

Fruit

God calls each of us to bear fruit in this world through our talents, skills, and blessings. That is the multiplication for the kingdom from people who once were sinners. Beautifully ironic, right? He uses the ones He knows have hope and faith in Him, the ones who truly know His healing hand, because He saved them from the bottomless pit.

There are worse things in life than death. Being without God's comfort or walking blindly is one. There is no direction, no answer, no truth. Doubt can come between us and how God plans to use us for His glory.

One day, while out running, I ran by a bush with beautiful red flowers, and I felt God speak to me. He asked, "See the ones withered and closed?" I acknowledged Him, and He said, "I cannot use them, for they are closed." Then He said, "See the ones that are blossomed? I can use them, and like them, I will use you." Unsure what to think about that, I kept running, and He asked me one more question. "Can you bear My cup?" God moves through this world, and His power is given to the servants, who will bring life to many who walk in death. There is no hope without Him.

People will search for things in this world that bring comfort or numb their pain. [1]Just look at statistics in 2015; 35 percent of

---

[1] T. W. Post, "Prescription painkillers more widely used than tobacco, federal study finds," Denver Post, September 20, 2016, retrieved May 1, 2017, http://www.denverpost.com/2016/09/20/prescription-painkillers-tobacco-study/Christopher Ingraham.

American adults, roughly one in three, were prescribed painkillers that year. That beats tobacco users by 4 percent, and we aren't even factoring in those who abuse pain pills. Of course, within those numbers, you can say some truly need painkillers. Knowing this fact, I like to suggest that those numbers are much higher than ever before.

This generation has tried to remove God from schools, television, and life. Every day millions search for happiness, but they don't find any. The earthly remedies can heal only temporary pain. Our God heals everlasting pain. Until we find Him, His love, and the forgiveness that gives rest to our sins, we will continue searching. You have nothing to lose in accepting Christ, but you gain everything. Sure, following Him can cost you so much in this world.

The key statement is "in this world." Think about this: you get maybe one hundred years on earth. Sure, you can live life at one hundred miles per hour, but will that fulfill you? Let me save you the time; no, it will only exhaust you. God created us in His image, and when we are separated, we aren't at rest. Life doesn't work. You might then ask, "Why doesn't God come down here and solve our problems or save us from death?" He did. He came as a baby, born to a virgin, and He lived as a man, died on a cross, and rose three days later as our Savior. Defeating the grave, He bears every one of our sins, fears, and evil ways. All He asks of us is to love others and bear fruit. To finish, this topic can be summed up in a story from Matthew 21:18–22.

> Now in the morning as he returned into the city, he hungered. And when he saw a fig tree in the way, he came to it, and found nothing thereon, but leaves only, and said unto it, Let no fruit grow on thee henceforward for ever. And presently the fig tree withered away. And when the disciples saw it, they marvelled, saying, How soon is the fig tree withered away! Jesus answered and said unto them, Verily I say unto you, If ye have faith, and doubt not, ye

shall not only do this which is done to the fig tree, but also if ye shall say unto this mountain, Be thou removed, and be thou cast into the sea; it shall be done. And all things, whatsoever ye shall ask in prayer, believing, ye shall receive.

He used this parable for His disciples. From afar, some believers' works look amazed, but closer examination would tell you the works are hollow and fall short. The sacrifices are weak, and the activities are few. Sincerely worshipping Christ and bearing fruit for the kingdom are necessary to be a follower of God. Religion with substance and nutrients will feed His people.

For this reason, I bow my knees before the Father, from whom every family in heaven and on earth is named, that according to the riches of His glory He may grant you to be strengthened with power through His Spirit in your inner being, so that Christ may dwell in your hearts through faith-that you, being rooted and grounded in love, may have strength to comprehend with all the saints what is breadth and length and height and depth, and to know the love of Christ that surpasses knowledge, that you may be filled with all the fullness of God. Now to Him who is able to do far more abundantly than all that we ask or think, according to the power at work within us, to Him be the glory in the church and in Christ Jesus throughout all generations, forever and ever. Amen.

(Eph. 3:14–21 ESV)

DAY 8

Facilitators

"These things have I written unto you that believe on the name of the Son of God; that ye may know that ye have eternal life, and that ye may believe on the name of the Son of God" (1 John 5:13). To be members of the community of Christ, we are facilitators for the kingdom of God. Giving a more sensible statement, I use this example. If I wanted to take a cruise to the Caribbean and wanted to know everything about my package deal, I would see a travel agent. He or she would facilitate the purchase. Then I would receive my package, after which I would travel to the boatyard.

Once I was there, I saw the ship captain, and he would ask, "Did you pay in full?"

"Of course I did! I received my package and have traveled very far and have been tested along the way."

"Then enter and enjoy your cruise."

In the example, the travel agent was a facilitator. The package was Christ, and the Captain was our heavenly Father. The short example is life, and I believe it started when we received Christ. Through facilitators, we are taught of His love and presence in the world. The receipt is paid in full, from the cross to the grave and three days later to the heavens. The ruler of all eternity gives grace to the world through the love of a Father. Without acknowledgment of Christ as our Savior, we will never see the eternal destiny our Father has laid out for us. Renewed by the blood of a broken body on an old, rugged cross, hell was defeated. "Jesus saith unto him, I am the way, the truth, and the life: no man cometh unto the Father, but by me" (John 14:6).

When Adam and Eve failed, God's foresight hinted of the coming of Christ. During His conversation with Satan, God said, "It shall bruise thy head, and thou shalt bruise his heel" (Gen. 3:15). He described Satan's defeat in the beginning. God hates sin, and sin leads to death, but without a perfect lamb for a living sacrifice, we couldn't have a personal relationship with God. As believers, we must facilitate the meeting with others so they can make a personal decision for Christ. From that point, it's on them and their dedicated journey, which allows them to board the cruise ship. For the facilitators, when asked how to accept Christ, remember this prayer:

"God, my Father, I am before You today, and I understand I am a sinner. Forgive me with Jesus's blood as He is the pure, living sacrifice for all the world. He came as a baby, born to a virgin, lived a sinless life, and died for everyone, defeating the grave. He rose again, taking our sins and washing them white as snow. Now I ask You to be my Savior. Live in me for all others to see. Jesus, I proclaim You as my Lord. Come into my life. From now on, I am Yours, and Satan's no more! Amen."

Put on then, as God's chosen ones, Holy and beloved, compassionate hearts, kindness, humility, meekness and patience, bearing with one another and, if one has complaint against another, forgiving each other; as the Lord has forgiven you, so you also must forgive. And above all these put-on love, which binds everything together in perfect harmony. And let the peace of Christ rule in your hearts, to which indeed you were called in one teaching and admonishing one another in all wisdom, singing psalms and hymns and spiritual songs, with thankfulness in your hearts to God. And whatever you do, in word or deed, do everything in the name of the Lord Jesus, giving thanks to God the Father through Him.

(Col. 3:12–17 ESV)

DAY 9

Calling

"I came not to call the righteous, but sinners to repentance" (Luke 5:32). Have you ever experienced an emotion that couldn't be understood or explained? Then out of nowhere, you could hear yourself talking to yourself? Now, before you say I'm crazy, remember that when God speaks, at times He resembles our voice. Some skeptics may say you are nuts, but if you experienced this situation, you know what I'm talking about, and I challenge you to listen. Remember, don't let ignorance fool you.

God will never tell you to do something that contradicts His commandments. If that is the case, then rebuke the thought; never take ownership of it or give it the light of day, because the angel of darkness is trying to fool you with his words. When God calls us to conduct the heavenly work He has especially planned for us, we are given knowledge beyond our understanding. This is why it's important to listen and pray over the things we cannot understand. The more we exercise the ability to listen to our Father, the more everything seems to make sense, and the more He speaks. "And he said unto them, Is a candle brought to be put under a bushel, or under a bed? and not to be set on a candlestick?" (Mark 4:21).

Our calling is to live for Jesus and understand the direction in which God leads us. Pleasing our Father could equate to the greatest victory of our lives. The blessings it will bring are irreplaceable. Also, what would be greater than hearing, "Job well done, my good and faithful servant"? That would be the greatest lifetime achievement award one could ever receive. So, I challenge you today. What is your calling for the kingdom? Which soil are you?

And when he was alone, they that were about him with the twelve asked of him the parable. And he said unto them, Unto you it is given to know the mystery of the kingdom of God: but unto them that are without, all these things are done in parables: That seeing they may see, and not perceive; and hearing they may hear, and not understand; lest at any time they should be converted, and their sins should be forgiven them. And he said unto them, Know ye not this parable? and how then will ye know all parables? The sower soweth the word. And these are they by the way side, where the word is sown; but when they have heard, Satan cometh immediately, and taken away the word that was sown in their hearts. And these are they likewise which are sown on stony ground; who, when they have heard the word, immediately receive it with gladness; And have no root in themselves, and so endure but for a time: afterward, when affliction or persecution ariseth for the word's sake, immediately they are offended. And these are they which are sown among thorns; such as hear the word, And the cares of this world, and the deceitfulness of riches, and the lusts of other things entering in, choke the word, and it becometh unfruitful. And these are they which are sown on good ground; such as hear the word, and receive it, and bring forth fruit, some thirtyfold, some sixty, and some a hundred. (Mark 4:10-20)

No weapon that is fashioned against you shall succeed, and you shall refute every tongue that rises against you in judgement. This is the heritage of the servants of the Lord and their vindication from Me, declares the Lord.

(Isa. 54:17 ESV)

DAY 10

Strength

When God uses strength, it may not be when we suspect it, or the time may not be when we would understand. Acknowledging this fact and knowing the event is beyond our control are necessary. This will allow Him to take control of the situation and use us to His fullest measures. More times than not, He brings strength when we are at our lowest point in life. This sets the stage for our willingness and acceptance of His gifts and blessings. The moments in life when we feel we don't have anything to lose is when some of His greatest works can be done. "That he would grant you, according to the riches of his glory, to be strengthened with might by his Spirit in the inner man" (Eph. 3:16).

God has great wealth that He is capable to spread throughout His people for His wonders. But through the Holy Spirit inside us, He will have granted great strength to exercise for His good. The untapped power at our disposal to defeat Satan and the sins that come with his ways are controlled by the key of faith. Faith unlocks the power of God, which starts with faith in Jesus Christ. Once we have accepted Christ and have the faith of David, we can move mountains in the name of Jesus.

David knew he would kill Goliath because of his faith, and just like his defeat of the bear and lion, David as a boy defeated Goliath. Years of repetitious Bible stories have numbed some of our minds to the true heavenly potential that surrounds us. Now understand that I'm not saying the stories are a problem. What I am saying is that we read them over and over, but when we experience God, the stories come alive. They become a reality, because God has taught us to defeat modern Goliaths.

The revelation we experience when God's calls us brings a whole new meaning to His truth, because we are exposed to His light and understanding. What an addiction it is to chase after

God's own heart because He chose you for one of His tasks. "But they that wait upon the Lord shall renew their strength; they shall mount up with wings as eagles; they shall run, and not be weary; and they shall walk, and not faint" (Isa. 40:31). In your darkest moments, God can bring you refuge and transformation. Believing He has the power to defeat the grave gives you the power to walk out of troubles and create ministry.

The aim of our charge is love that issues from a pure heart and a good conscience and sincere faith.

(1 Tim. 1:5 ESV)

DAY 11

Love

And thou shalt love the Lord thy God with all thine heart, and with all thy soul, and with all thy might. (Deut. 6:5)

And he answering said, Thou shalt love the Lord thy God with all thy heart, and with all thy soul, and with all thy strength, and with all thy mind; and thy neighbor as thyself. (Luke 10:27)

Jesus left us with many words, and He lived a perfect life. He demonstrated the greatest act of love in human history. "Greater love hath no man than this, that a man lay down his life for his friends" (John 15:13).

The word *Christ* is roughly mentioned 555 times in the Bible, and the word *love* is roughly mentioned around 551 times. In its pages there is a direct message of Christ and love. God is love, and He commands us to love, yet most of us fail to show this in our actions. I would like to challenge you to see how your day will go if, deep down inside when you see people throughout your day, you say, "I love you in my head and believe it." I will tell you that by lunch you will be so overjoyed that the stressors of life will be forgotten. This world will come and go. The secret's out; you will be too.

If people remembered you for one thing, would it be love? We praise God when we love others unconditionally. "This is my command, That ye love one another, as I have loved you" (John 15:12). He didn't give an option or alternative to this. Just love. What is the one thing people will die for? Love. It is the most powerful tool we have as Christians, because if we love, others will be attracted to us. The truth of love is that we didn't choose Him; He chose us. He chose love so our end would have another possibility other than certain death but everlasting life. Love is the pathway because it was the whole reason He died for us. He loved us so much and wanted to ensure that He was the last living sacrifice to clean us of our sins. Now we have His love living inside each of us, waiting to be set free.

If you know death is certain, why live life working toward it. Live to love and be loved; keep your loved ones close and celebrate life. You get only one life on earth, so practice love now because heaven brings love for eternity. It is unconditional.

Be still before the Lord and wait patiently for Him; fret not yourself over the one who prospers in his way, over the man who carries out evil devices! Refrain from anger, and forsake wrath! Fret not yourself; it tends only to evil. For the evildoers, shall be cut off, but those who wait on the Lord shall inherit the land.

(Ps. 37:7-8 ESV)

DAY 12

Stress

Has stress ever made you want to cry out and say, "Just take me now. I am so done with this"? At one time the chosen people of God also cried out this way. One month after God led Moses to bring His people from the hands of Egypt, they complained of hunger and told God they would have been better off if He had killed them when they were in Egypt. "He brought us to the wilderness to starve us," they said.

This story is all too familiar in our lives. Everything is going well, and then out of nowhere, we are hit with tragedy or the test of our strength. Instead of leaning on the Father and asking Him to bear our cross with us, we complain and give up. Nothing stops our true potential faster than stressing uncertainty, which leads to weakened faith. Can you imagine an army of trained professional soldiers chasing you? Just as they trap you in front of the ocean, with nowhere to go, God moves. His almighty power spreads the sea like an open book. God moves. But we are so soon to forget His mighty works when faced with that imaginary wall of troubles.

Could you understand for one second what God must see? Looking down on us, He sees us making mountains out of mole hills. He must look down on us and think, *Are you kidding me? I just moved an ocean for you, and now you need food? You can't figure that out with the God-given talent I gave you?* He showed the people of Israel they were too quick to complain. He made the manna rain down from the heavens, and His people ate. God moves.

Stressing about life is a powerful tool used to stop revelation in our lives. It starts so small, but through imagination and Satan's lies, it grows out of our control. We just gave control to the son of darkness and missed what God was going to show us. The next time you face uncertainty, realize this burden will pass. God moves. "He only is my rock and my salvation: he is my defense; I shall not be moved. In God is my salvation and my glory: the rock of my strength, and my refuge, is in God. Trust in him at all times; ye people, pour out your heart before him: God is a refuge for us. Selah" (Ps. 62:6–8).

These things I have spoken to you, that my joy
may be in you, and that your joy may be full.

(John 15:11 ESV)

DAY 13

Joy

Just as Satan brings stress to our lives to distract us from our true
potential, God brings us joy. He allows us to taste a fraction of
what we will experience in heaven. We can have overwhelming joy
for all eternity. No pain, no sickness; not even death exists where
the Father calls home. He is preparing a place where our fruits can
be displayed for all eternity. It's a place where love exists between
all who share His space. Understanding that there is a resting
place after this world is finished brings joy of understanding and
a desire to live by His principles. Ever wonder why God or Jesus
uses phrases with joy in it? It is heavenly, but this earth cannot
contain the joy of heavenly proportions. It can only taste it.

Sometimes in human nature we miss heavenly gifts. Know
that love, joy, and peace aren't of this world. Think about love,
for instance. In love, we experience joy and peace. In peace, we
know love and joy. In joy, we know peace and love. Connections
with God can be missed so easily when we aren't focused on Him.
If we start our day in Him, we can achieve everything our hearts
desire but also see it through a lens of love, peace, and joy. Not
only will we have a better day but a day of nourishment. Growth
in the Father is there since we are living with Him and He in us.
"Blessed are the poor in spirit: for theirs is the kingdom of heaven"
(Matt. 5:3).

I cannot grasp the fulfillment of the Father's blessings, but
what I can express is that nothing else matters when we have it.

It is like a lightning strike from heaven, and it's to die for, because true happiness is discovered in Him and His joy. "Therefore my heart is glad, and my glory rejoiceth: my flesh also shall rest in hope" (Ps. 16:9).

For His invisible attributes, namely, His eternal power and divine nature, have been clearly perceived, ever since the creation of the world, in the things that have been made. So they are without excuse.

(Rom. 1:20 ESV)

DAY 14

Uncertainty

"I will go before thee, and make the crooked places straight: I will break in pieces the gates of brass, and cut in sunder the bars of iron" (Isa. 45:2). *The New Oxford American Dictionary* defines *"uncertainty"* [2] the state of being uncertain: "doubt" [3]. Under the synonyms portion, the dictionary takes the word to a further description. It describes *uncertainty* as something that lacks conviction. So how do we expect God to move in our lives if we live in uncertainty?

How many times have you prayed with uncertainty and hoped for a miracle? How many prayers have been unanswered in your life, a result you chalked up in a statement like, "Well, I guess it wasn't His time"? I know I am guilty of this. God does have His timing; I don't disagree with that, and your time doesn't even compute to His. But remember, it starts with us and our belief. Then God can start His move. What God hears in moments of uncertainty is that hope is lost and faith is nonexistent. It never even left your environment. How do we expect it to enter God's? How many prayers were left floating in thin air because we didn't believe they were fulfilled when we first prayed.

---

[2] *The New Oxford American Dictionary, s.v "uncertainty"* 3rd e.d, June 10,2017

[3] *The New Oxford American Dictionary, s.v "doubt"* 3rd e.d, June 10,2017

The New Oxford American Dictionary defines *"certainty"*[4] as something that is known for sure, and beyond doubt. The beautiful truth of God is certain. Arguably, He is the only thing certain in this world. When looking at the definition of *uncertainty*, I can't help but imagine the path traveled in *uncertainty* with a Father who is certain, who will lead us to His truth. It's faith that keeps us moving, and it's God's love that guides us like a light in darkness. We cannot be blind when we see the Father. His light is knowledge; His way is certain, and His truth is life. We haven't begun to live until we see Him as the way, the truth, and the light. "I had fainted, unless I had believed to see the goodness of the Lord in the land of the living" (Ps. 27:13).

---

[4] *The New Oxford American Dictionary, s.v "certainty"* 3rd e.d, June 10,2017

No one who abides in Him keeps on sinning; no one who keeps on sinning has either seen Him or known Him.

(1 John 3:6 ESV)

DAY 15

Sins

"Keep back thy servant also from presumptuous sins; let them not have dominion over me: then shall I be upright, and I shall be innocent from the great transgression" (Ps. 19:13). To understand the crippling aspects of sin, we must define it in its entirety. *Sin* is anything that defies our maker, is destructive to His nature, is completely separated from His will, and breaks His commandments. Our time frame and understanding of time in this life allow the opportunity to challenge God.

If we strive to not live in sin, then why is it possible to sin at all? Being captured by life's priorities and our blindness to see the light amongst darkness, sin can be destructive. Sometimes different paths take us to unforeseen places, and through sin light can be produced. This doesn't mean sin is intended to happen for His will to be followed through. But through conviction, we can repent and walk from it. This allows for closer relationships to the Father and an understanding like the prodigal son's father had when his son returned.

Like the prodigal son's father, our Father opens His arms to us when we return. We come back to Him with a stronger understanding of life and His love. In return, we are blessed. Some of the hardest lessons we learn in life come through the pain produced and endured from a decision we made. After the storm, we are much wiser and become better facilitators. This is because we have experienced the pain shared by others we try to witness to. Our understanding of their struggles establishes comfort and a future for them. They also see at that moment that God has made us whole. This is something they will be looking for, the comfort that can come only from God and His love. The book of Job, a great example of a hard lesson learned, opens a greater understanding of our Father, His love, and His wisdom.

So faith comes from hearing, and hearing through the word of Christ.

(Rom. 10:17 ESV)

DAY 16

Faith

And the head of Ephraim is Samaria, and the head of Samaria is Remaliah's son. If ye will not believe, surely ye shall not be established.

(Isa. 7:9)

Beloved, when I gave all diligence to write unto you of the common salvation, it was needful for me to write unto you, and exhort you that ye should earnestly contend for the faith which was once delivered unto the saints. For there are certain men crept in unawares, who were before of old ordained to this condemnation, ungodly men turning the grace of our God into lasciviousness, and denying the only Lord God, and our Lord Jesus Christ.

(Jude 1:3–4)

I was listening to a podcast, and two individuals were talking about the differences between Islam and Christianity. The lady being interviewed wasn't a great debater, and she found herself in an uneasy situation. Trying to get out of the corner she'd backed herself into, she said, "Isn't it great how Christianity has lost some of their radical views? All religions are becoming more contemporary with the times, and they are evolving with age."

I remember thinking, *If that is true, we are failing.* The Bible is the guide we should follow, and it's older than anyone living today. So how are we becoming this new, hip, modern religion? Are we appeasing the people around us and changing our views to be modern? I pray not. I would argue that the church that is succeeding has adapted to the times, but the doctrine has stayed the same, not the doctrine of theology but the Holy Spirit-led message of God. What I mean is that the colleges have directed the institutionalized theology. Many new pastors have been called by God, but they are not theologians.

Great people go to Bible colleges every year. I think that is marvelous, but are we being taught how to perceive God instead of how to know Him? No college can give you a God-led experience. You have to chase Him like David did. Interestingly enough, the Bible mentions David almost as much as it mentions Jesus Christ. I believe the man had it right with his approach to God. I understand that many would disagree with my statement, but God has led me to make the observation in this book just as He asked me to write it. We need faith today more than ever.

We need a community where churches are helping each other instead of competing with each other. The mission is the same. Who cares how one operates and another doesn't? If people are being saved, why does the approach matter? Those are your brothers and sisters.

I challenge the pastors of today. If you're a modern pastor who rocks the church like a concert, find a pastor who is a theologian; and if you're a graduate of a Bible college, find a pastor who isn't. Together you can make waves for Christ. But be warned; if you bend the rules our Father set to appease the masses, you are a false teacher and aren't in His will, for the black-and-white text on the pages of God's word shows His words men wrote for a heavenly purpose. Christ spoke the red words.

One thing I hear over and over is that men wrote the Bible, men with God living in them. These were powerful revolutionists for all generations, inspired by God. They weren't taught how to study, for they knew the love of "I AM." His love led them like a lantern on a dark path, and because of them, we have a book today that has never been destroyed or wiped off the map. If the Bible was of man, why would we still have it today? Many books come and go, but God's word will live forever.

My flesh and my heart may fail, but God is the strength of my heart and my portion forever.

(Ps. 73:26 ESV)

DAY 17

Temptation

Woe unto the world because of offences! For it must needs be that offences come; but woe to that man by whom the offence cometh! Wherefore if thy hand or thy foot offend thee, cut them off, and cast them from thee: it is better for thee to enter into life halt or maimed, rather than having two hands or two feet to be cast into everlasting fire. And if thine eye offend thee, pluck it out, and cast it from thee: it is better for thee to enter into life with one eye rather than having two eyes to be cast into hell fire.

(Matt. 18:7–9)

So many things in this world can lead us to failure. Failing God who knows unimaginable love can lead us to redemption. He has made us in His image and inspires us to live Christlike lives. Temptations are examples of where the thief of life or the king of darkness can move in a facet we cannot understand. When you feel temptations, you must ask, Why does Satan want me to stumble? What is going on in my life to explain why he has targeted me? Satan knows your temptations and understands how to pick your brain to find the most desirable things in your life. He exploits these ideas or thoughts and uses them to maximum potential. You must push away from him or fail in your daily walk. I wish I could tell you there's an easy way out, but there isn't. The only way to release these desires is to lay them at the cross with Jesus. Allow God to carry your heavy burden for you.

Why do you think the devil showed Jesus the kingdoms of the world during the tempting of Christ in the wilderness? They are the only kingdoms the devil will ever experience. These kingdoms of the world never belonged to Satan in the first place. Jesus understood that these were His Father's kingdoms, and He defeated Satan using God's words. The devil wanted to be worshipped and saw this as an opportunity to carry out his plan. But by Jesus's refusal, He was able to redeem the world and pay the ultimate price for our sins. Jesus is the key to our temptations, and He is the way to success in our walk with the Father. Jesus spoke the word and knew it wouldn't return void, knowing it is alive.

And what is the immeasurable greatness of His power toward us who believe, according to the working of His great might that He worked in Christ when He raised Him from the dead and seated Him at His right hand in heavenly places, far above all rule and authority and power and dominion, and above every name that is named, not only in this age but also in the one to come.

(Eph. 1:19–21 ESV)

DAY 18

Power

A power plant is capable of distributing power to thousands, yet still it cannot reach everyone. A hydroelectric dam can distribute power to many, yet it still falls short of every home. How is it that Christ is known and worshipped in every country in the world but electricity still fails to reach everyone? The power of Christ continues to keep the lights on in our hearts, even in times of shame. He never lets us go without Him.

He that is not with me is against me; and he that gathereth not with me scattereth abroad.

(Matt. 12:30)

But he said, yea rather, blessed are they that hear the word of God, and keep it.

(Luke 11:28)

The limitations of life come from our inability to serve the Father wholeheartedly. Our intentions must be true, and minds need to be clear, for we cannot drag our old selves around to call on when we may or may not need them. That portion of us is gone, and it has been slain through the power of Christ.

If you call on your old ways, you are working against the very calling that will make you great. Ask the Father to give you great power for His kingdom, and He will. Be ready for this, because the devil will be your enemy, and he will use your own mind against you. Covering yourself with God's anointment and living for Christ will set you free. Don't worry about Satan. He has already been defeated, and it is he who defeats his own objectives, for he plays chess with God daily. But unlike God, he is blind to Christ's next move. If you live in darkness, you cannot see light.

That which we have seen and heard we proclaim also to you, so that you too may have fellowship with us; and indeed, our fellowship is with the Father and with His son Jesus Christ. And we are writing these things so that our joy may be complete.

(1 John 1:3–4 ESV)

DAY 19

Fellowship

My brothers and sisters in Christ, know we are called to unite and worship our Father with great love. Adoration for the Father is grace and glory. The days are growing closer to our final ones, and every day we are called to worship the One who gives us light. Without light, we are dead, and in darkness comes true evil. Would worship look different if you were taken from life and revived back to it? Or if you lost something dear to you, and it was given back when all hope was lost? Then I ask you—take a look at being born again and consider the process.

He loved you enough to save you from a runaway train and place you back on safe ground. He pulled you from certain death in a deep darkness. He placed you in His light. How can you even repay a just God? Through a yearly revival? Through three weeks of devotions—just walking away when your life gets busy? Maybe a post on your favorite blog dedicated to your life? Where are the dedication and humility of His people? He wants you to be a child on fire for His love. He wants to host your accolades in the highest, above many. His fellowship gives great power and rejuvenation to your spirit.

Today many dedicate their actions and achievements to anything except His glory. I cannot understand how we must look in front of Him with so much of our lives dedicated to us.

This world must be a great place with every picture and post being so happy and staged. I would argue that there are so many who have beautiful social media pages, but I'm still saddened because they want more. What's missing are the fellowship and warmth of God's love. They are what we search for every day but seem to miss. They are right in front of us. We find them in Him. "The grace of the Lord Jesus Christ, and the love of God, and the communion of the Holy Ghost, be with you all. Amen" (2 Cor. 13:14).

My charge to you is to let go and be free. Accept what He has provided for you and know love. I don't have an issue with social media, and I believe it has connected the world in a way nothing in our lifetime has as yet. It has been used for good, but it has also destroyed our focus and reality of what is important. It consumes our time. When we wake up and before we go to bed, priority is to post and read others post to our favorite social media sight. Replace those times with God, and blessings will be abundant. Life is astronomically bigger than a social media page.

For He was crucified in weakness, but lives by the power of God. For we also are weak in Him, but in dealing with you we will live with Him by the power of God. Examine yourselves, to see whether you are in faith. Test yourselves. Or do you not realize this about yourselves, that Jesus Christ is in you? Unless indeed you fail to meet the test! I hope you will find out that we have not failed the test.

(2 Cor. 13:4–6 ESV)

DAY 20

Spiritual Mind-set

Why is it, in this day and age, that our community of faith is so quiet about God? Do you think that in most churches, people who need healing, whether spiritual or physical, actually receive it? Could it be that most people going to church are trying to be blessed rather than to bless the kingdom? When was the last time you told a stranger how much the Father loves him or her? Any day now, Christ is returning. Time measured to us isn't the same length of time to Him, because He already knows the time of Jesus's return. So what calculation can be done if you already have the time and place in which you arrive preplanned and marked on the internal calendar?

God looks down on us and sees everyone focused on everything else but Him. How can we expect miracles for the kingdom to be done in people's lives if this is how we portray Him? God intends us to enjoy our lives, but He wants us to enjoy Him and what He brings to our table. If you are worried about how others will perceive you, let me be honest. People who are close to us will be lost due to our relationship to Christ. Here is the truth; as we assist Him in mighty works, He prepares a kingdom for us. Your works aren't of this world. Your works feed a much higher cause. Our mind-sets are the leading cause of our spiritual failures. We pray for miracles, but in our minds, we don't believe they are done. Yet we expect God to move.

Here is an example: I stay up all night and never prepare for my exam. At the last minute, I tell the teacher I need to pass this, or I'm not going to graduate. If you're lucky, you will produce anything other than a failing score. Now you may say, "That example doesn't really correlate." You're missing the point. Neither act gets past step one. Next time you ask a favor of the Lord God Almighty, Creator of heaven and earth, Father to a crucified Son, Father to a lost world, ask yourself, *What have I done for Him?* I'm not perfect by any means, not even close.

What I can tell you is that this is amazing. When you love people and support the kingdom, your life will forever be changed. *Addictive* isn't expressive enough. Paul wrote in 1 Corinthians 12:28 about the appointed positions in the church. "And God hath set some in the church, first apostles, secondarily prophets, thirdly teachers, after that miracles, then gifts of healings, helps, governments, diversities of tongues." If we cannot even understand how the church is supposed to be set in place, how can we perform almighty acts of the kingdom? Why could our Lord perform miracles and raise the dead two thousand years ago but we cannot in this age? Let me hit you with the red letters from the Bible in John 14:12–14. "Verily, verily, I say unto you, He that believeth on me, the works that I do shall he do also; and greater works than these shall he do; because I go unto my Father. And whatsoever ye shall ask in my name, that will I do, that the Father may be glorified in the Son. If ye shall ask any thing in my name, I will do it."

Jesus never did miracles on demand; He was not a magician. His miracles were strategic for the kingdom and allowed a connection from heaven to earth so many could be saved. If I wanted to pray for someone who battles an addiction to alcohol, I would pray for him or her to be healed from the addiction for the testimony it will bring for God's kingdom and His will for the person who was healed. Look past the problem you're praying for and look toward the objectives of God.

But put on the Lord Jesus Christ, and make no provision for the flesh, to gratify its desires.

(Rom. 13:14 ESV)

DAY 21

Lust

Lust, a broad term that can be defined as anything manmade or not, is something desired more than anything else. It is a desire you long for so bad, and it will drive you mad the longer you go without it. It is not limited to a nature expressed in sexual immorality, but it is idolatrous in design, feeding manmade desires. These are the hidden addictions we either share or keep tucked away in our minds, the exact place where Satan lurks.

If you were a general planning a war campaign, would you turn your plan over for the other side to use in your demise? We all do this over and over, myself included. We are new creatures in Christ, taking off the old and placing on the new. We keep fighting the good fight. The longer we resist temptations, the stronger we get. Combining this technique with the scriptures and with how Jesus leads an example for us to follow, we can succeed. Sometimes I feel as if I have failed Christ so many times in this category. The thing I want to capture is the moment He says to me, "You're still fighting. Your desire for me is getting stronger. Keep fighting."

Standing at the finish line, there He'll be, cheering for me until that day comes. The race I run, every step, is one closer to kingdom come. "Mortify therefore your members which are upon the earth; fornication, uncleanness, inordinate affection, evil concupiscence, and covetousness, which is idolatry: For which things' sake the wrath of God cometh on the children of disobedience" (Col. 3:5–6). In your time of struggle, lift your head and understand that because He lives in you, your heart is love. Where anger once lived, mercy now takes its place. The power of His bloodshed on that day thousands of years ago equated to rivers of baptism and conversions of our old nature to His. It is the barrier we must pass through from our world to our Promised Land—from barbarism to sanctification. We must leave our baggage at the cross so He can facilitate God's work through us.

Remember the word that I said to you; A servant is not greater than his master. If they persecuted Me, they will also persecute you. If they kept My word, they will also keep yours.

(John 15:20 ESV)

DAY 22

Relationships

I understand the importance of knowing your history and where your family has come from. Displayed through so many different channels are the commercials for web- based companies that provide ancestry services. I know the general background of my family through grandparents, and I remember the stories told in front of the fireplace on many holiday occasions. But why has this interest started such a large-scale movement to define everyone?

In today's age, we need fewer lines of division and more relationships with our brothers and sisters in Christ. It feels like this tool of lineage data is used as a tool for how some should live. Learning twenty minutes ago that you are from a Scottish immigrant born in 1895 shouldn't make you want to start wearing a kilt to work. It doesn't define your behavior. You are what God has chosen you to be. I've seen famous men and women on TV find out their great-grandparents or someone in their family was a slave owner. Then they proceeded to apologize, but for what? Are you going to let the past evils determine who you are today? No! You can't, or it will be a tool of Satan's destruction.

History bears its share of pain—no question about it. We learn from failures and mistakes to become great. Maybe what we need now and forever are the relationships of God, close friends, and future Christians. Have you ever met a Christian who was so consumed in his or her interpretation of faith that he or she wouldn't associate with nonbelievers? It boggles my mind every time I hear this. My church, while I was growing up, asked a homeless man to leave because the elders didn't want him to be a distraction. I would argue that their selfish behavior to a child of God caused even me to leave the church mentally for about twenty years. There were hundreds there that day. One action could have turned hundreds away.

Let me call out to all those who feel they should be missionaries. Really, here's an easy step to practice. Go buy some hamburgers at your favorite fast-food chain and hand them out to the homeless. The training you will get in one hour will teach you so much about the meaning of life. The homeless are so broken beyond repair; they will challenge every word, but with tears in their eyes, an unconditional "love cheeseburger" goes much further than the price you paid for it. That cheeseburger was bought with the blood of Christ, and from one broken body to a broken soul, repair begins. Ten dollars will get you access to someone, who before would have spat on you or cursed you. I pray that God would give them unconditional love in each bite.

I remember one occasion; there was one man I talked to, but he wasn't having anything I said. He kept smashing his cheeseburger, then taking a bite. Each bite, bite by bite, his eyes watered. I held my expressions inside, because even though he disputed every word I said, he felt love. I could see it. After thirty minutes, he couldn't take his experience anymore and took off, but I would like to think God hasn't let up on him.

Relationships are found around every corner. Whom will God put in your life to challenge your walk and strengthen it at the same time? Jesus went to where the sinners were and fellowshipped among them. He ate with the tax collectors, even though He was looked down on for doing so. Sometimes we are called to dangerous situations for the betterment of Christ. We must walk among wolves as sheep in wolves' clothing. This will give us access to a population that rebukes Christ. Through our relationships with nonbelievers, we will grow, and they will come to know His will. Remember, you have Christ on your side. How can they possibly hurt you? Did God not close the lions' mouths when Daniel was in the lions' den? He is the same God; He is the same now as He was then. "Let your light so shine before men, that they may see your good works, and glorify your Father which is in Heaven (Matt 5:16).

What kind of relationships will you establish today?

But for this purpose, I have raised you up, to show you My power, so that My name may be proclaimed in all the earth.

(Ex. 9:16 ESV)

DAY 23

God's Power

The power of God lives every day inside us. We must understand how to tap into it. Starting with God's will for a desired action, this power will be known through His voice moving inside us. It will challenge our abilities to do something we may or may not want to do. Normally, the unexpected happens after we show our bravery to follow Him. He will use us to move mountains in someone's life. Second is our personal belief that God's power is truly potential in this world. His divine glory will set the conditions for the facilitators to move in His almighty ways. Third is expressing the action in Jesus's name through the Son; this brings glory to the Father. We must be full of godly confidence, because adding doubt brings Satan into the recipe, and he can shut this down. He isn't more powerful than God.

It's our doubt in God that makes the Father question us. This will limit His moving through us. You may ask yourself, why would He do this? The answer is easy; He will find someone in His mighty sea of people to use for the same thing He asked of you. You see, He doesn't need us in this spectrum; we need Him. We must want to bring people to Him and make others' pain flee. We must look at the person who curses and spits in our faces and say, "Brother or sister, I want to walk in heaven with you."

Let me give you some examples of how He has moved in my life. Remember the "unconditional cheeseburgers" from the last entry; the homeless man who almost cried as he ate the cheeseburger was moved. God moved, but what I didn't tell you is that the other

49

homeless man there was so filled with Christ that he instantly started countering the teary-eyed man. He took what Jesus had given me to say and ran with it. That man had stage-three cancer and a bad heart. He had nothing to lose. Jesus found him on his cross, which he was carrying. We prayed that night for God to heal him of his cancer and heart problems, and without a shadow of a doubt, I know that man is healed. Now God has a man with a larger target audience on the streets who can preach to a group who have been forgotten. He has proof through his healing, because the other homeless people have seen him leave the streets in an ambulance many times before. This is bigger than us. He taught us to fish for a reason.

One morning I woke up feeling full of His mercy. I prayed, "God let everyone I encounter today know I belong to You, without even saying a word." I believed this, but as my day grew busy, I forgot that I had prayed this prayer. I was in the grocery store and shopping for the week. What I couldn't understand was why those who saw me went from experiencing whatever they felt to being filled with happiness and joy. I remember looking at the first couple of people and watching as their frowns and stern looks turned to pure happiness. I was a bit confused, but then I remembered what I had prayed. I was taken aback so much. I could see it in their eyes, because they looked at me like I had a unicorn horn growing out of my forehead and was literally stopping them in their path.

People, He moves through us, and this is powerful. Just saying, "Hi" to someone when we are having a God-filled day could stop someone from suicide, because the person may feel the very thing he or she couldn't experience before: love. These are your brothers and sisters. They need you. Some cannot handle life, because they live without purpose in God. They live in shadows, and we question why preventable death happens. Crazy thing is, we have the power to stop it. Remember, God's will and timing aren't for us to decide. We must have faith, even when we don't witness the healing right away. God has the time and place where He will move. We facilitate His movement. Exodus 3–4 provides a great example of how God calls us to facilitate His plan.

For we are His workmanship, created in Christ Jesus for good works, which God prepared beforehand, that we should walk in them.

(Eph. 2:10 ESV)

DAY 24

Model Christian

How do you sum up the title "Model Christian" into words? I can't define that for you, because I'm not sure a definition exists. By placing that word combination into a subject, I believe it limits us from the start. For more structured individuals, I will give you this answer to define it. Who am I to question God? When He talks to you, remember that phrase. There will be many challenges that won't make sense, such as Peter's eating with Gentiles. In that time of our world, his diet wasn't proper. "And the voice spake unto him again the second time, What God hath cleansed, that call not thou common" (Acts 10:15).

When you become a Christian, it's all about God. You must remove what defined you before and look to the heavens for your new proclamation, for He has created you, a new creature, and you are now to go forth and bring the dead to life, walking a Christ like life for others to see in you. They will desire your presence and what you possess. The Bible doesn't say to go forth and proclaim everyone's faults. It doesn't say to tell others without Jesus, "You don't deserve happiness." The answer is to love everyone and do so abundantly. People may think you're crazy until you show them your nature is a blessing from divinity.

The Bible may be old, but it has all the secrets you desire. It's your guide to live a Christian lifestyle. He gave you the Holy Spirit. You must understand this; the Holy Spirit is the very spirit that placed Jesus in a virgin. You have great power and responsibility. God requires you to be an example of Him. You are His workmanship.

Love one another with brotherly affection.
Outdo one another in showing honor. Do not be
slothful in zeal, be fervent in spirit, serve the
Lord. Rejoice in hope, be patient in tribulation,
be constant in prayer.

(Rom. 12:10-12 ESV)

DAY 25

Connections to God

Prayers hit heaven faster than the speed of light. What happens to the ones that don't seem to get answered? First, we must know that a genuine prayer must come from the heart and that not all needs are truly needs in the eyes of God. This is like praying for a car to provide for your family physically when you can't afford one. Or it's like praying for a new SUV because your three-year-old SUV isn't new anymore. Don't represent yourself like that to God; a lot of us are guilty of doing option two. It's disrespectful to His nature and shows our earthy instinct to chase worldly things.

But what about true needs, true heart-filled prayers that fall short? I will tell you that one option is our faith. The other are His timing and purpose for unanswered prayers. If you pray for someone with cancer who truly needs prayer but in your heart lack faith in His almighty wonders, unfortunately the prayer may fall short. Prayer in itself is an act of faith. I want you to know there could be many reasons for a prayer to go unanswered. It happens. But since prayer is an outward and inward display of our faith, how can God possibly use our prayer if we don't believe in His abilities? I would argue that the prayer may even fall into evil hands, because our faith is wavering like the tides of the sea, tossed back and forth. It may even be used to highlight our unwillingness to believe that God's work is being done.

When I pray, I like to believe it is done and complete. I just wait for the Father's timing. It's like the old infomercial: "You have to set it and forget it." Now, we shouldn't forget it, but we should send it and believe God has answered it, whether that be tomorrow or twenty years from now. That isn't for us to decide. May His will be done on earth as it is in heaven, plain and simple. Don't get in the way of God and His abilities to act. "Therefore I say unto you, What things so ever ye desire, when ye pray, believe that ye receive them, and ye shall have them" (Mark 11:24).

Jesus said to him, "If you would be perfect, go, sell what you possess and give to the poor, and you will have treasure in heaven; and come, follow Me." When the young man heard this, he went away sorrowful, for he had great possessions.

(Matt. 19:21-22 ESV)

DAY 26

Rejection

Why is it easy to reject Christ? Why is being a Christian perceived in a negative manner? Why is it so easy for Satan's trickery to fool us? Why don't we believe in God's love?

I know this is why so many finish the race called life without anything to show for it. You may have had millions of dollars, but what did those buy you? Did you buy yourself a nice coffin? "Blessed are the poor in spirit: for theirs is the kingdom of heaven" (Matt. 5:3). Is it because we can so easily trade earthly pleasures now versus waiting on heavenly ones? Is it because we worry what flesh will think of us? What about how God perceives us? "Draw nigh to God, and he will draw nigh to you. Cleanse your hands, ye sinners; and purify your hearts, ye double minded. Be afflicted, and mourn, and weep: let your laughter be turned to mourning, and your joy to heaviness. Humble yourselves in the sight of the Lord, and he shall lift you up" (James 4:8–10).

What an honor there must be to be proclaimed a good and faithful servant of Christ and to hear the Father say, "Great job. Welcome home." Until the public acceptance of our Lord, so many will reject Him. That may seem harsh, but failure to recognize your sins in front of the Master is false hope. The blood of Christ spilled on the cross is the direct lineage for us of our relationship with God and the sins He alone can wipe clean. Sins are the very things that separate us from Him. Jesus, the true carpenter, built the bridge between us and God; we just have to walk across. "Blessed are they which do hunger and thirst after righteousness: for they shall be filled" (Matt. 5:6).

Therefore, my beloved brothers, be steadfast, immovable, always abounding in the work of the Lord, knowing that in the Lord your labor is not in vain.

(1 Cor. 15:58 ESV)

DAY 27

Thoughts

"But Peter and John answered and said unto them, Whether it be right in the sight of God to hearken unto you more than unto God, judge ye. For we cannot but speak the things which we have seen and heard" (Acts 4:19–20). Stand firm in the word of God. It is your guide in life, and everything you seek is in this mighty book. Be cautious of false prophets, for they existed in the past, and they will come in the future. Remember that our God will never contradict His work or commands. Beware of the ones who claim the works of God but proclaim His glory for themselves in their actions. We are just the ones who facilitate His will or His miracles.

We cannot take credit for something that is of Him. He is able to work through us because we have faith and strive to live lives for Christ. The ones who exalt themselves as holy and greater than most aren't of the Father and are most likely false prophets. We are just men and women, made of flesh and bone. God is the Alpha and Omega, the beginning and the end. He is the reason we have life.

We must have a bold approach when it comes to spreading the good news about our Lord, for He humbled Himself enough to come as a man, God in the flesh, to live a perfect life and be a sacrifice for our sins. Without this open display of love, we would never have our connection to God. Our boldness is the joy He pours into our lives, because we know there are greater things to come. We are the winning team. The last chapter of this world has been written. The secret is in the book of Revelation, and we will be victorious. Hell was defeated when Jesus was crucified and broke the grave. As He descended to earth, He then ascended to heaven. "Him that overcometh will I make a pillar in the temple of my God, and he shall go no more out: and I will write upon him the name of my God, and the name of the city of my God, which is new Jerusalem, which cometh down out of heaven from my God: and I will write upon him my new name. He that hath an ear, let him hear what the Spirit saith unto the churches" (Rev. 3:12–13).

My son, keep My words and treasure up
My commandments with you; keep My
commandments and live; keep My teaching as
the apple of your eye; bind them on your fingers;
write them on the tablet of your heart.

(Prov. 7:1-3 ESV)

DAY 28

Bible

The Bible, our daily guide, the guidance from our history as Christians, the definition of our belief it is what stand for and who we become in Christ. The book itself is just paper and ink. It's when we combine it with the meditation with our Father that it begins to be understood. When we come to Him in worship and prepare for His presence, we tell Him we are ready to go where He is going to take us. We prepare for the presence of God, our Creator, to have a personal moment with us. I'm not sure how we miss this.

Have you ever read the Bible and thought, *This is hard to interpret*? The book is written in our language, but yet it's like it's not. Then you come back after worship and being still with the Father and listen. The same verse takes you in depth to what He wants to share with you. You look at it in confusion that you missed the simple gospel. Unlock your hearts; stop putting a time frame on the Lord.

I get it; lives are busy. Sometimes I work up to eighty hours a week. I have a family of five, and I am a part-time college student. Life will deal you a hard hand if you let it. Sacrifice a little sleep for the Master, and He will give you true rest. He is jealous for you. Imagine what He will give you when you tell Him, "You first, God, today and every day." "He must increase, but I must decrease" (John 3:30). I challenge you today to sacrifice part of your day for

Him and see where this step takes you. It will be a journey you will never regret. We ask for miracles, yet what have we done for Him? It starts with worship. That is the start of this journey.

While the earth remains, seedtime and harvest, cold and heat, summer and winter, day and night, shall not cease.

(Gen. 8:22 ESV)

The Lord by wisdom founded the earth; by understanding He established the Heavens; by His knowledge the deeps broke open, and the clouds drop down the dew.

(Prov. 3:19-20 ESV)

DAY 29

Earth

"It is he that sitteth upon the circle of the earth, and the inhabitants thereof are as grasshoppers; that stretcheth out the heavens as a curtain, and spreadeth them out as a tent to dwell in" (Isa. 40:22). Ever wonder why life on earth can never be perfect? Even your most memorable day has its fair share of imperfections or joyful events you look back on with laughter. Just when you think it could never be better, something unexpected occurs. Life's imperfections make us look to His glory and think of how great heaven must be, a place where not even one aspect is imperfect or ugly. Not even someone's thought is of an ill nature.

Our earth is as good as it's going to get. Nothing we can do will change how we look at this world in the aspect of the shell we live in. Sure, we can do things to make it better, but in our last days, the earth is still the earth. It's beyond our control, and there are way too many moving pieces for us as humans to perfect it. There will always be an unexpected change or something in the equation of earthly life that kinks our long- running intentions. We can do so much with our free will, but acceptance of the earth, that it is what it is, and heaven as the end state is victory.

This discussion makes us think about how our efforts should be focused, whether we pursue heavenly goals or earthly ones. Everything we do is to the pleasure of God, and we should care for our home, because He provided it. Our life here on earth is one that should be pleasing to Him. We should try to be the best at what He has asked of us. But our focus is always on Him and His plans for us. My grandfather wrote in his Bible, "God First." This was his reminder that no matter what his plans were for the day, God was first in his life through prayer, meditation on God, and worship. Begin your day in God's light and watch your day transform. Day by day God notices as you chase after His light, and He will fill you with His glory.

No one has ascended into heaven except He who descended from heaven, the Son of Man.

(John 3:13 ESV)

DAY 30

Heaven

"In that I command thee this day to love the Lord thy God, to walk in his ways, and to keep his commandments and his statutes and his judgements, that thou mayest live and multiply: and the Lord thy God shall bless thee in the land whither thou goest to possess it" (Deut. 30:16). In life the key to our finish is the way we live for Him. Perfect lives can be sought after, but Jesus was and is the only perfect form of man to ever walk this earth. This should mean we will strive for a walk like His. The Bible affirms that we must seek to walk in His light and ways. This will reaffirm our drive to victory, and our grand finish for the kingdom will be strong and abundant, firmly standing for the life of Jesus through knowing and understanding His gift to us. He has His ability to never leave or forsake us, even though He left this world to sit at the right hand of God.

When He took His place in His kingdom after His death, He never left us. He provided the Holy Spirit to guide us in our walk, which mimics the dynamic lifestyle He lived. He strategically gave us the Holy Spirit, the lifeblood of this world. He remains in us as our Comforter. The Holy Spirit gives us the light from Jesus and keeps us on a path to heaven. This is achievable, because the Spirit has freed us from our sinful nature through the power of Christ. His death affirmed our glory on the day we finish our race called life. "For as many as are led by the Spirit of God, they are the sons of God" (Rom. 8:14).

The journey we are asked to take in the life of a Christian

believer is long and hard. Not only do we battle the world and its earthly ways, but we battle our own minds against our sinful desires. Like Abraham, we also can confidently look forward to a city designed by God, where His Son rules over His house as the High Priest, and the presence of God is among us all. Till that day, we will live in faith and love.

Jesus answered them, "Truly, truly, I say to you, everyone who practices sin is a slave to sin."

(John 8:34 ESV)

DAY 31

Fault

Paul said, "For we know that the law is spiritual: but I am carnal, sold under sin" (Rom. 7:14). God's law after our transformation to Christ is evident and clear. The quiet conscience and brevity are our new guide to life, telling us when actions are right and wrong. Satan and all his tricks challenge us to stumble. We are now subject to the conviction of our sinful natures. Before, we weren't disturbed by our sins, but after we accepted Christ and received the Holy Spirit, our eyes have been opened. Like the blind seeing for the first time, we see the true nature of man. Temptations never felt so strong; evil never felt so close. Like the smell of death, its presence lurks over us. When we lose to sin, our fight has lost momentum. We have suffered a devastating blow, and weakness grows. Our addiction, to sin, holds a tight grasp that in our failure Satan laughs in our defeat. We have placed our Lord and Savior on the cross.

How can we overcome the very nature that consumes us? This is the addiction that came before all substances of dependency, and that is sin. "O wretched man that I am! who shall deliver me from the body of this death?" (Rom. 7:24). When life is opaque, Jesus clears our vision. Your mind, after accepting Christ, wants nothing more than to obey God by doing what He has deemed right. It is the new nature of your Spirit. The rebirth of Christ in you strives for righteousness. When our faults lead to failures, they linger in us like a newly born stench. My friends, there will be times when you fail and never understand how or why. Control and will power to overcome the sinful desire you crave cannot be replaced overnight. Our life in Christ is a lifelong journey and teaching. He walks daily with us as a mentor, and through the Holy Spirit, He is our guide. Our failures will be few, but accept that there will be some. Pray for forgiveness, lift your head up, and focus on the Father, for it is He who has already forgiven. For what your mind doesn't understand is that His almighty ways have already made you whole again. Because He knew your beginning, He also knew your end.

As for you, always be sober-minded, endure suffering, do the work of an evangelist, fulfill your ministry.

(1 Tim. 4:5 ESV)

DAY 32

Prayer

The beauty of prayer, other than the conversation that takes place, is the representation of faith between you and God. The Father already knows what you are going to pray for, but the covenant of faith is the sealer that holds the bond. Wait patiently for the Father, for what He intends to do with our request, and for His natural way to mold us through our experiences in Him. What are the intentions of our prayers, and how do we prepare before we come to the Father? We should come to the Father as a child and talk freely; there is no disagreement there.

At times I think we can be more capable of hearing the Father than when we come prepared for His presence. Finding a quiet place and enjoying Him privately are the very things Jesus was talking about in Matthew 6. What an amazing representation of our King's humble nature, for which He allows us to be in His presence. This is a true testimony of His amazing grace and humbling love. But preparing a time and place to worship and pray to our Father will pay dividends in our relationship with God. "Offer the sacrifices of righteousness, and put your trust in the Lord" (Ps. 4:5).

It is pleasing to God when we make an effort for time with Him that is well thought out and planned. Before your daily prayer time, take time to be in private worship. Allow the rush of the day and the many tasks that need to be completed fall to the side, clearing your mind of an earthly thought process. Allow for clarity and peace, just you and the Father, together in the right spirit. Many times Jesus went away privately to be with His Father, as should we. It is a daily renewal in the Father and sets the conditions for placing on our full armor of God. His gift to us ensures the preparation for our daily battles.

After this manner therefore pray ye:

Our Father which art in heaven,
Hallowed be thy name.
Thy kingdom come.
Thy will be done in earth,
As it is in heaven.
Give us this day our daily bread.
And forgive us our debts,
as we forgive our debtors.
And lead us not into temptation,
but deliver us from evil:
For thine is the kingdom, and the
power, and the glory, forever.
Amen

(Matt. 6:9–13)

In whom are hidden all the treasures of wisdom and knowledge.

(Col. 2:3 ESV)

DAY 33

Wisdom

"For wisdom is better than rubies; and all the things that may be desired are not to be compared to it" (Prov. 8:11). Ever think about wisdom as an entity? Could you image it as a senior adviser to the world? The Bible states, "When he prepared the heavens, I was there: when he set a compass upon the face of the depth: When he established the clouds above: when he strengthened the fountains of the deep" (Prov. 8:27–28). The thought of it is very interesting when you put Solomon's words into context. It is very interesting how he set the stage in Proverbs 7 by warning immoral women and their deceptions of portraying wisdom as a sister.

"My fruit is better than gold, yea, than fine gold; and my revenue than choice silver" (Prov. 8:19). Such a beautiful statement is also ironic since possessing great wisdom can produce wealth. She provided both for those who ask and seek her knowledge, for she lives with good judgment so that common sense and success belong with her. Life's foundations structured under wisdom are the cornerstone of life itself, for building your house with a solid foundation creates an undisturbed fortress for all life's challenges.

On the topic of wisdom, Solomon's advice is to love her like a sister and let her protect you from an affair of an immoral woman. Wisdom provides true guidance, and like the immoral woman who tries us in temptation, wisdom is present and real while instructing us to look past her deceptions and keep on walking. If we listen, we will be wise and prosper. If we fail, we will have been another victim. Solomon stated, "She has been the ruin of many"; there is so much more to these chapters other than the lessons of man and woman. Satan lurks on every corner just like an immoral woman waiting to capture another in her snare of life.

But when the goodness and loving kindness of God our savior appeared, He saved us, not because of works done by us in righteousness, but according to His own mercy, by the washing of regeneration and renewal of the Holy Spirit. Whom He poured out on us richly through Jesus Christ our Savior, so that being justified by His grace we might become heirs according to the hope of eternal life.

(Titus 3:4-7 ESV)

DAY 34

Kindness

To know God is to understand love and the fullness it can provide. To know love is to understand kindness and the genuine spirit it gives. Maybe for years we have been looking at the equation of our lives all wrong. I would argue that life equals love plus kindness. It's when we add other variables that we set our conditions against God's will, not knowing what He has for our equation. When we add the equation of life in our daily walk with Christ, His true nature is radiant, and our portrayal of Him is evident. We are given a chance in this world to commit our lives to the Father, and through His kindness, we are saved. He does this not because of who we will become or the great deeds we will do but because He is kind. He is love. He knows mercy. In the Bible, love and kindness go hand in hand. There is no mistake in this, because love and kindness coexist, and in kindness is love. Inarguably, you cannot have one without the other, for how can you love without being kind? Likewise, how can you be kind if you don't love? "He that loveth not knoweth not God; for God is love" (1 John 4:8).

God is love; He gave us Jesus and not only as representation of heaven on earth, but as a living sacrifice through His kindness, we are saved. His kindness in us is our representation to the world. This is what causes people to want to know more about our Father. Feeling the kindness that makes us warm is sought after all over this world. Be an example for others, and they will know Him through you.

What is man that you are mindful of him, and
the Son of Man that you care for Him.

(Ps. 8:4 ESV)

DAY 35

Man

Man was designed in God's image for the purpose of His will to
be carried out. Man from day one was given a task and a free
will. Just as God warned Adam not to eat from the tree of good
and evil, He allowed Adam's free will to choose life or death. This
truth is still relevant today in our decision in Christ. He still gives
us our free will to choose earthly pleasures over the treasures of
His kingdom, to walk fulfilled in Christ or man.

What will truly sustain our lives? God breathed life into Adam
for His purpose, but the beauty of it all was allowing Adam to
choose God. The same choice is made every day on earth. No
matter the sins of your past, you have found Him, and now freely
you can allow Him to live inside you forever. This is the beautiful
relationship of His design.

No matter how far or how long one chooses to live without
Him, a free person chooses at the pinnacle point to reverse his or
her ways and follow Christ. "The first man is of the earth, earthy:
the second man is the Lord from heaven. As is the earthy, such are
they also that are earthy: and as is the heavenly, such are they also
that are heavenly. And as we have borne the image of the earthy,
we shall also bear the image of the heavenly" (1 Cor. 15:47–49).

One day our form, which is man, will be removed. We will be
given a new form that is perfect for our life with God, and our
new form will be like the spirit of Christ, one suited for the eternal
life we are promised. "For there is one God, and one mediator
between God and men, the man Christ Jesus; Who gave himself
a ransom for all, to be testified in due time" (1 Tim. 2:5–6).

On one of those days, as He was teaching, Pharisees and teachers of the law were sitting there, who had come from every village of Galilee and Judea and from Jerusalem. And the power of the Lord was with Him to heal.

(Luke 5:17 ESV)

DAY 36

Healing

The power in healing is so impressive; even today thousands seek its mercy. When Jesus preached, many would reach out just to touch His garments, because of the healing power that flowed from within Him. "And now, Lord, behold their threatening's: and grant unto thy servants, that with all boldness they may speak thy word, By stretching forth thine hand to heal; and that signs and wonders may be done by the name of thy holy child Jesus" (Acts 4:29–30).

When we talk in the boldness of Christ, we too can bring the power of healing to others through the heart of God and His love. Trusting in our Lord and Savior brings healing to us and gives strength to our souls for His greater good. For if we are to bring healing to others through Jesus's mighty power, we must have healing from the Father for ourselves. What do we say to someone in need if we give without asking in return? How does someone understand our actions when we provide for him or her out of love? To heal hearts that have been hardened, we must soften them with God's love. Healing is unconditional and unprofitable.

For true healing power to take place, we must set the venue for God's work to take place. This starts with being a servant for others and ends with not profiting from our actions to another. God profits in these situations, and His rewards will be great. But beware of the human nature inside you. We must be careful and understand that the power within us is from God and not of us or this world. He gives us power from heaven to heal. The power starts from loving God with all your heart, soul, and might. Don't allow His powerful healing to have earthly side effects. Go with love and show others through Jesus that you have been healed.

To me, though I am the very least of all saints, this grace was given, to preach to the Gentiles the unsearchable riches of Christ, and to bring to light for everyone what is the plan of the mystery hidden for ages in God who created all things, so that through the church the manifold wisdom of God might now be made known to the rulers and authorities in heavenly places. This was according to the eternal purpose that He realized in Christ Jesus our Lord, in whom we have boldness and access with confidence through our faith in Him.

(Eph. 3:8-12 ESV)

DAY 37

Boldness in Christ

Life is fast paced, and before you know it, morning becomes night. The fast-food industry has capitalized on speed versus quality for years. The food isn't always better for your health but fast enough to get you back to your daily life. Like health, our spiritual lives can suffer from a fast-spiritual diet. Take time to understand that God will ask us to set aside time for Him; this is key to our growth in a healthy walk. To be bold in Christ starts with devoting time to Him daily so His mentorship can begin. Accepting that personal sacrifice for Him is much better than receiving from another. To know the boldness in Christ is to serve others with joy and love. "For even the Son of Man came not to be ministered unto, but to minister, and to give his life as a ransom for many" (Mark 10:45).

Third is living with humility and humbleness. The Savior of all mankind, one week before He was crucified, rode into Jerusalem on a colt. Humbled and all knowing, He was the Messiah who would save His creation. He came before the world as a King, born in a manger, a carpenter by trade; and He died a criminal's death as a perfect sacrifice for us.

To be bold in Him, we must understand the bitterness of His cup. He was baptized in suffering so we will know life. He provided us a means to life; we just need to understand what comes from it. We must be prepared to "fight the good fight," as Paul would say. This world will take everything from you if you let it. Stay focused on the Lord, and He will go forth and guide you as the light of life. He can make the blind see, and it is He who can give us understanding of our hardships we are to bear, because He has carried it all.

And I saw the beast and the kings of the earth
with their armies gathered to make war against
Him who was sitting on the horse and against
His army. And the beast was captured, and
with it the false prophet who in its presence had
done signs by which he deceived those who had
received the mark of the beast and those who
worshiped his image. These two were thrown
alive into the lake of fire that burns with sulfur.

(Rev. 19:19–20 ESV)

DAY 38

Beast

"And he said unto them, I beheld Satan as lightning fall from heaven. Behold, I give unto you power to tread on serpents and scorpions, and over all the power of the enemy: and nothing shall by any means hurt you. Notwithstanding in this rejoice not, that the spirits are subject unto you; but rather rejoice, because your names are written in heaven" (Luke 10:18–20).

The mighty accuser of transgressions has played his tricks on this world for a long time. His days are numbered, and his time is near. He knows this, but his simplistic skills to play chess with the Father proves his inability to foresee our future actions. If Satan had understood what Jesus's death meant to life, would he have allowed him to die? God is always multiple moves ahead of Satan in this world. This truth is easy to understand, because, as Jesus stated, "Behold, I give unto you power to tread on serpents and scorpions, and over all the power of the enemy: and nothing shall by any means hurt you" (Luke 10:19).

We are the only things that give power to Satan, whether through our imaginations of him, lack of confidence in ourselves, or even worse, our lack of faith. And sadly, even our spoken words give Satan power when used in lack of faith. Satan will trick and tempt you just as he tried with Jesus in the wilderness. Our power against him is with the word of God just as Jesus used it. This is why it's so important to hide God's words in our hearts and be ready for battle when needed. It's evident that the Beast cannot keep up with God's work.

Remember, God's word is sharper than a two-edged sword. When we speak the Father's word, Satan has to flee. Satan wanted to be God, but he failed to see the Father's divine plan through Jesus's sacrifice. Lucifer told Jesus to bow before him, and he would give Jesus all the kingdoms of the world. The great secret was that the kingdoms already belong to Jesus, because in the beginning He was with "I AM" When do we stop giving evil the power over our lives? He is a weak coward; we have the strength of heaven's armies over us. Be strong in the word and understand its measures, because it is sharper than a two-edged sword, capable of piercing any armor of the evil one. God's desires for your life are stronger than Satan's doubts.

Do not marvel that I said to you, "You must be born again. The wind blows where it wishes, and you hear its sound, but you do not know where it comes from or where it goes. So, it is with everyone who is born of the spirit."

(John 3:7-8 ESV)

DAY 39

Born Again

When we see death, thoughts of negativity and pain come to mind. But when God sees death, He sees rebirth and new beginnings, for death can defeat us in the grave only if we have never accepted Jesus. This life is precious and short, but it allows us time to prepare for life after death. The afterlife is where God's eternal promises come to life. God's love and kindness are the reasons we are saved. You can never do enough good in the world to be acceptable to heaven. Only through the Savior are we made righteous. It is His grace that allows our exit from earth and our acceptance to eternal life. "Jesus answered and said unto him, Verily, verily, I say unto thee, Except a man be born again, he cannot see the kingdom of God" (John 3:3).

Jesus came to earth, sacrificing everything heaven had to offer. For thirty-three years, He walked this earth as a perfect Lamb, teaching the world of heavenly things. He did this because God's love for us is greater than our earthly imagination. He sent us a Servant not to judge the world but to give light. The Son of Abba gave us everything, but people still choose darkness over light. Love for evil is greater than love for our King. The ones who choose the Father give a radiant light that many find disgusting, for the fear of their sins being exposed is greater than their desire for redemption.

Our acceptance of the Lord and Savior is truth for all who

don't know Him. They see what we are doing and how we act, so we must be careful in our ways. Nonbelievers will hold us accountable for every stumble in an attempt to disprove the existence of the One we fear. Their fear is simple, for they know what they do, and they know their wrongs. To be born again, we must be born of the spirit and water. Our mothers and fathers created life, but the Holy Spirit gives birth to spiritual life.

If then you have been raised with Christ, seek the things that are above, where Christ is, seated at the right hand of God. Set your minds on things that are above, not on the things that are on earth. For you have died, and your life is hidden with Christ in God. When Christ who is your life appears, then you also will appear with Him in glory.

(Col. 3:1–4 ESV)

DAY 40

I Am

Be still, and know that I am God: I will be exalted among the heathen, I will be exalted in the earth.

(Ps. 46:10)

Jesus said unto them, Verily, verily, I say unto you, Before Abraham was, I am.

(John 8:58)

And God said unto Moses, I AM THAT I AM: and he said, Thus shalt thou say unto the children of Israel, I AM hath sent me unto you. And God said moreover unto Moses, Thus shalt thou say unto the children of Israel, The Lord God of your fathers, the God of Abraham, the God of Isaac, and the God of Jacob, hath sent me unto you: this is my name for ever, and this is my memorial unto all generations.

(Ex. 3:14–15)

When I think about the word *eternal*, I imagine several things: something that is unchanging, valid for all time, forever. I consider ideas such as expressed truths, values, and the idea of something without beginning or end, Alpha and Omega. Have you ever wondered what it must have been like before God created everything? How did something come from words spoken into existence? I believe this question is the boundary for a lot of nonbelievers; the answer is essentially belief without seeing proof. When you personally decide to believe in Christ Jesus, you have to wonder how it all began and the very essence of the decision. It is faith. I mean, where did God come from? The only answer I can put into context is, He is everything; He is endless.

Your personal decision is a choice, the one solely up to you. You can think of this as a privilege in this world that He provides us with. It was a key to an eternal door, in which we can choose the light or the dark; but either way, the choice is ours. Just as the snake deceived Eve, the first couple were given a choice in the beginning. God commanded them not to eat from the tree of good and evil, because it would lead to an outcome that was much greater than they could have ever imagined.

The ability to choose Jesus is the beauty and honor God gives us to choose life over death. This keeps our faith from being empty. It gives us light to the reason we totally rely on Him. Without choices in life, we would be mindless and meaningless. What would be ours in a world without a choice? He has always given us the choice and the possibility of the wrong decision. He uses our mistakes to strengthen our resolve and as a means for us to grow through hardship. It is His design for us to choose Him freely. "And unto Adam he said, Because thou hast hearkened unto the voice of thy wife, and hast eaten of the tree, of which I commanded thee, saying, Thou shalt not eat of it: cursed is the ground for thy sake; in sorrow shalt thou eat of it all the days of thy life; Thorns also and thistles shall it bring forth to thee; and thou shalt eat the herb of the field" (Gen. 3:17–18). This choice cost Adam and Eve the ability to reside without cost in the garden as "I AM" originally chose for them. Let us not give into desire but ask of the Lord what His purpose for our lives is.

And when they saw Him they worshiped Him, but some doubted. And Jesus came and said to them, All authority in heaven and on earth has been given to Me. Go therefore and make disciples of all nations, baptizing them in the name of the Father and the Son and of the Holy Spirit, teaching them to observe all that I have commanded you. And behold, I am with you always, to the end of the age.

(Matt. 28:18-20 ESV)

DAY 41

God's Authority

The authority that lives within us is the same authority that placed God's Son on the cross to ensure our redemption. He provided the way through Him, the truth about life, and the light that cannot be put out. "And he said, Therefore said I unto you, that no man can come unto me, except it were given unto him of my Father" (John 6:65). It is puzzling, but we still think we are in control in this life after the events that led up to Jesus's death. Even though Jesus knew His end on this earth, He still expressed His agony to the Father. Jesus understood that God's will should be done and not His; He knew the control was the Father's. "Saying, Father, If thou be willing remove this cup from me: nevertheless not my will, but thine, be done" (Luke 22:42).

If the Father's authority wasn't love, would Jesus's sacrifice have been necessary? He created us in His image, and after Adam and Eve ate from the tree, He foreshadowed Jesus's victory over darkness. His authority over this world will be completed as simply as the seasons change. God will replace this world of evil and renew the life He intended for us prior to the deceit in the garden of Eden. He will renew us in a heavenly image for all eternity, a day He has patiently awaited. And yet we ourselves have no patience.

What an amazing Father we have. Like the number of servants who will join Him is His understanding that the day and the hour are known to Him and only to Him. His authority reigns daily, and our actions represent this or contradict it. Our actions are in preparation for His will after this world is over and His work is complete, just as baptism represents new birth in Christ from spiritual death. We will rise from the grave, being brought back from the dead to a new form. Jesus was chosen to be the first to represent His Father's authority in this defeat of the grave. Everything has a purpose in the realm of God's will. Jesus will be given supreme authority over all except God, who in the end will defeat death so we can live for all eternity. Thank You, Father.

And we know that the Son of God has come and has given us understanding, so that we may know Him who is true; and we are in Him who is true, in His Son Jesus Christ. He is the true God and eternal life. Little children, keep yourselves from idols.

(1 John 5:20 ESV)

DAY 42

Clarity

"Whom God hath set forth to be a propitiation through faith in his blood, to declare his righteousness for the remission of sins that are past, through the forbearance of God; To declare, I say, at this time his righteousness: that he might be just, and the justifier of him which believeth in Jesus" (Rom. 3:25–26).

Our Father demonstrates His divine purpose without failure. He has foreshadowed the plan of a perfect sacrifice since the day of Adam and Eve's failure to obey. Since that day of the first sin, God has had a plan for our rescue from the depths of hell. We have to recognize His purpose in us and see that a Lamb was given as the final sacrifice for all to come. His grace understood that people of times past didn't have the opportunity to see the coming of His Lamb, and He showed mercy on them.

The divinity of our Father is incomprehensible in our minds and inevitably causes our doubts at times. Clarity with the Father starts when we receive Jesus as our perfect sacrifice. It grows as we long to learn and receive wisdom our Father provides us to do His work. One thing that made Abraham and David so special in God's eyes was their continued and relentless faith in God. They counted on Him for everything, and if called, they were ready to give everything in His name. Their clarity came from the commitment proved throughout the actions that represented the Father well. God forgave their sins because of their faith, not because of good deeds.

Our clarity day to day is knowing a Father who loves and enjoys our company, Someone who is always there with open arms, welcoming us in His presence. His plan for us has always been a deeper relationship; He has proved this in His plan for our eternity. It's always been about us and His love for His creation. From the day of separation, when Adam and Eve ate from the tree, until now, He has always had a plan to reunite us in heaven. Clarity comes in His divine ways, that He is coming for us one day to bring us home.

Come to Me, all who labor and are heavy laden, and I will give you rest. Take my yoke upon you, and learn from Me, for I am gentle and lowly in heart, and you will find rest for your souls.

(Matt. 11:28-29 ESV)

DAY 43

Rest

"Let that therefore abide in you, which ye have heard from the beginning. If that which ye have heard from the beginning. If that which ye have heard from the beginning shall remain in you, ye also shall continue in the Son, and in the Father" (1 John 2:24).

Our rest is from the Father and His ability to give us the relaxation our spirits need to refrain from becoming dull. At times we get so caught up in our daily lives that God asks us to take a step back and look at our beginning in Him, remembering the passion created from a renewed mind to spiritual knowledge and understanding that comes only from faith. Our faith and the constant requesting His guidance show our growth but also our belief that He is the sole provider for our lives. No matter how amazing the path is that He takes us on or the journey of finding Him daily, He asks that we never forget the beginning that brought us to Him. This is a check and balance to ensure we prosper and grow spiritually. "For what if some did not believe? Shall their unbelief make the faith of God without effect?" (Rev. 3.3).

Our rest is knowing Jesus died for us through the sacrifice of a perfect Lamb so we can access our Father, a Father who wants nothing more than to receive His people on the day He calls each of us home. Keeping our eyes focused on Him will allow His guidance and wisdom for all our actions. This assurance brings rest for every decision in our lives and the comfort that He is leading our every move. Through rest is growth, and how great it is to keep our eyes on Jesus to ensure He will never surprise us like a thief in the night on that day He comes back for us. "I know thy works: behold, I have set before thee an open door, and no man can shut it: for thou hast a little strength, and hast kept my word, and hast not denied my name" (Rev. 3:8).

Our lives are a representation of not only Jesus but also the sacrifice He gave for us, for if we cannot love each other, then how do we understand a love that cost a perfect life willfully given for the world that was created through Him? Jesus came to earth to serve, not to be served. He is patient with us, so we must have patience for others. This is a representation of His grace. His blood purchased our bounty to death. Rest assured, we have an inheritance like no other waiting for us, an inheritance like no other. In Him we shall receive a rest necessary to renew our spirits from battle and life's trials, knowing He promised never to leave us or forsake us. He left us with a guide to live with us. Our guide is the Holy Spirit, God within us.

And it shall come to pass afterward, that I will pour out My spirit on all flesh; your sons and your daughters shall prophesy, your old men shall dream dreams, and your young men shall see visions. Even on the male and female servants in those days I will pour out My spirit. "And I will show wonders in the heavens and on earth, blood and fire and columns of smoke."

(Joel 2:28-31 ESV)

DAY 44

Supernatural

There is no question throughout history that our God has moved in ways earthly minds cannot understand. He has such a way of developing everlasting understanding in others who see the trails He places along our path. We cannot question Him or fall to self-pity. His divine understanding of our strength is a light others need to see. Our trust in Him during our hardest moments will succeed, because our faith during these events was in Him. Through our testing, others can explain our success only as divine in nature. The little things God will ask of His chosen to endure inadvertently will enable others to see the proof that our God lives.

King Darius proclaimed to the world that our Father was to be feared across the world. He is a God of mercy, and He saved Daniel from the jaws of the lions. Daniel's position facilitated God's word, which spread across King Darius's kingdom. This came about not from Daniel's high position in the government but because he stayed faithful to the Father even in certain death. The supernatural event that occurred in the den was a unique way God showed His power to prove to King Darius that He reigns.

Daniel was a true servant of God, and even though he may

not have understood what God was doing, his trust in the Father never faltered. I can only assume Daniel felt great joy after he noticed God's work through him. "He delivereth and rescueth, and he worketh signs and wonders in heaven and in earth, who hath delivered Daniel from the power of the lions" (Dan. 6:27).

We may not understand what God is doing in our times of trial. Keep your eyes on Him like Daniel did and pray for assistance so that through us His will may be done. Jesus completed His ministry to the world in thirty-three years. His ministry at times will take us a lifetime to understand it completely. Heaven's supernatural can easily be missed in the earth's simplest moments. But His supernatural events will continue to happen in miracles today and even before the great and terrible day of the Lord.

Therefore, the Lord waits to be gracious to you,
and therefore He exalts Himself to show mercy
to you. For the Lord is a God of justice; blessed
are those who wait for Him.

(Isa. 30:18 ESV)

DAY 45

Justice

Justice used the cross as a measurement to judge all who have sinned against the Father. Because this world was created through Him, His sacrifice was the standard by which everyone will be judged. Through justice comes the One who is "just," giving His judgment equally and firmly. Christ brought true understanding of love, goodness, and happiness for the world to see clearly without barriers. Our Father wants us to desire His presence and understand His role in our lives. God first. "Because he hath appointed a day, in the which he will judge the world in righteousness by that man whom he hath ordained; whereof he hath given assurance unto all men, in that he hath raised him from the dead" (Acts 17:31).

Through His compassion we should turn away from our sinful lives and focus on Christ while ensuring we aren't judging others based on their actions. How can we judge others who falter when we have our own secrets to present to our Father? "Who will render to every man according to his deeds" (Rom. 2:6). It isn't for us to expound upon the faults of others in their stage of life. God will see all on the day of judgment, because He is everything and everything is with Him. "I tell you that he will avenge them speedily. Nevertheless when the Son of man cometh, shall he find faith on the earth?" (Luke 18:8).

This justice will be true justice, granting eternal life or a second death. Everyone whose name isn't written in the Book of

Life will fall short of His glory. "And I heard a great voice out of heaven saying, Behold, the tabernacle of God is with men, and he will dwell with them, and they shall be his people, and God himself shall be with them, and be their God" (Rev. 21:3). He looks forward to welcoming His people home, declaring a job well done, for they traveled long and hard; this is not through their deeds but in their desire to keep their eyes on the Father, whom they will see in the end. Believing in His truth and following His ways, we will experience His light.

Thus, says the Lord: The people who survived the sword found grace in the wilderness; when Israel sought for rest, the Lord appeared to him from far away. I have loved you with an everlasting love; therefore, I have continued my faithfulness to you.

(Jer. 31:2-3 ESV)

DAY 46

Intimacy

Like a bridegroom, He courts our minds and hearts.
His vision is placed in our lives, guiding
us to achieve His divine plan.
He is the reason we ingest key nutrients
needed to sustain our spirits.
Without Him our journey is nothing more
than loneliness and despair.
He gave us the world to manage alongside
Him; we fail to see our authority given.
Our body is His chosen temple; our hearts are His home.
He created the world all around us, but
daily we overlook His miracles.
It's not until we are deeply suffering that our
eyes are open to His splendor, His grace.
Like a friend, He chose death to give experienced
life as Author of servanthood.
His leadership defeated our deepest fears; He gives us peace.
His control paves our road, but our earthly
minds keep us blind to His path.
Let go. Give in to Him; He is our torch when the stars are dim.
He navigates us through certain circumstances,
boldly teaching us life's design.

With Him we are fearless, even when we face our graves.
His teachings give us certainty that defeats
our fears; we have seen the story's end.
His daily walks are the food our soul needs; the
teacher of the soul leads us to eternity.
He never leaves or forsakes us when our eyes are laid on Him.
Like a child we depend on Him for every meal;
His love is nature and gives us shelter
In the midst of a weary world; He gives knowledge and wisdom.
Pain has no hold on His people; it is a temporary
situation that leads us to rest.
His eyes are always on our minds, a Shepherd
who always watches His flock.
Our tongues are His representation, either
loving or foul; we show our depth.
When He is distant, we have to ask, What
have we done? Why are You afar?
He is always with us; sometimes He decides
to be quiet, to bring us back to Him.
Walk us through life to show us Your love; our actions are not
the test, but our desire for You separates us from the rest.

Jesus said to the them, "I am the bread of life; whoever comes to Me shall not hunger, and whoever believes in Me shall never thirst."

(John 6:35 ESV)

DAY 47

Believer

"Now the God of hope fill you with all joy and peace in believing, that ye may abound in hope, through the power of the Holy Ghost" (Rom. 15:13). The Holy Spirit is the linkage that connects us to the Father and our divine inheritance. When we accept His Son as our personal Savior, He rests within each of us. No depth of sin can keep us from Him as long as we care and listen to what we are instructed through the Holy Spirit. He has gifted us the teacher, who should be treated like a single compass on a long journey.

There is something precious about our Creator wanting to have a personal relationship with each member of His flock. He bestows us with His great power, the same power that resurrected Jesus from the grave and prepared His throne. No condemnation awaits believers who depend on their Father. The ones who long to spend time getting to know Him and safeguard His commandments will be recognized as His chosen ones. He made us complete with Christ and set us free from our sinful nature; He gives us the mind-set of Christ. Our choice is simple; it is willfully choosing Him above all other distractions in this world.

The consistent ones who seek Him and revere His wisdom will join His kingdom, our eternal glory; just as He prepared Jesus's throne, He prepares our home. "No man can come to me, except the Father which hath sent me draw him: and I will rise him up at the last day" (John 6:44). We are new creations developed unto Jesus because our Father drew us to Him. In this act we are made right with God, washed clean and forgiven as

God's masterpiece. We are identified as belonging to our Father, because we have been gifted with the Holy Spirit and blessed with His spiritual blessings. This is possible only because Christ purchased us through the cross. What makes a believer different from a nonbeliever? A believer lives to satisfy the Father and conducts his or her life to follow His plan through the guidance of the Holy Spirit.

Nonbelievers live to satisfy their desires so they can boast loudly about their success. They don't live for the Father, not by His commandments, because they don't possess God's Spirit. They live by their instincts, wandering through life, which will never give true satisfaction or accomplishment. They cannot see that short-term accomplishment is vastly different from the completeness only God can give us. True success in this world includes knowing our Father, experiencing the Holy Spirit, and striving to live a life Jesus would recognize.

My God, my God, why have you forsaken me? Why are you so far from saving me, from the words of my groaning? O my God, I cry by day, but you do not answer, and by night, but I find no rest.

(Ps. 22:1–2 ESV)

DAY 48

God's Silent Moments

"Then said Jesus unto them, When ye have lifted up the Son of man, then shall ye know that I am he, and that I do nothing of myself; but as my Father hath taught me, I speak these things. And he that sent me is with me: the Father hath not left me alone; for I do always those things that please him" (John 8:28–29). There are moments in life when God is distant from us. He chooses to be far away for our growth or because we are in need of repentance. When we feel His presence is distant from us, we must analyze His alienation. Is it because of our behavior? Is He testing our walk when He isn't close? Would the Father be afar because we are growing in strength and He wants to solidify our spiritual maturity? Strategically, He removed the physical barrier between us and Him on the day of Jesus's crucifixion. So, for what purpose would He take a step away from us at key stages in our walk?

We must understand that when we feel His detachment, He is only a step away. He will never leave or forsake us. Jesus shared such pain in Gethsemane, not because death was imminent but because He knew our sins would be His first and only spiritual separation from His Father. "And about the ninth hour Jesus cried with a loud voice, saying, Eli, Eli, lama sabachthani? that is to say, My God, my God, why hast thou forsaken me?" (Matt. 27:46). This was Jesus's cross to bear for each of our sins. He had to be separated, for without His separation we wouldn't have a future in the kingdom. Hell is an extreme experience for one to be put through, but the flame is what everyone fears. Yes, the flame would be unimaginable, but separation from the Creator of this universe would be even worse to imagine, for our Creator is true love, and without love, you will experience true hell. Torture isn't feeling the love or warmth only the Father can provide. True hell is being alone and blind to our Father's nature.

Remember how short my time is! For what
vanity, you have created all the children of man!
What man can live and never see death? Who
can deliver his soul from the power of sheol?

(Ps. 89:47-48 ESV)

DAY 49

Time

"Woe to you who desire the day of the Lord! Why would you have the day of the Lord? It is darkness, and not light, as if a man fled from a lion, and a bear met him, or went into the house and leaned his hand against the wall, and a serpent bit him. Is not the day of the Lord darkness, and not light, and gloom with no brightness in it?" (Amos 5:18–20 ESV). Our time in our earthly bodies can be short in duration compared to a lifetime in eternity. The free will we are given from a God who gifted us with the ability to choose or reject Him will determine our end. What sorrow awaits those who never accept the Savior as the redeemer of all?

How terrible will the darkness of hell's properties be, a place so solitary your own conscience wouldn't recollect your name? There your ray of hope is lost; He is at the right hand of the Father. Judgment is complete, and you're alone for all eternity. It is a lonely palace of terror, if only you had time; time holds no ground in a place where minutes don't exist. The worst punishment of all is to never bear fruit again. Like a withered fig tree, all chance for potential nourishment has passed. "I am the vine; you are the branches. Whoever abides in Me and I in him, he it is that bears much fruit, for apart from Me you can do nothing. If anyone does not abide in Me he is thrown away like a branch and withers; and the branches are gathered, thrown into the fire, and burned" (John 15:5–6 ESV).

Life's seconds are carefully considered on the day we are

created, and none of us comprehends how and when it is complete. Our Father understands the measurement of time He provides our eternal clocks. The beauty of life is His design, which gives us the free will to find Him. God's power can heal the blind, but those who refuse to see cannot turn to Jesus and be healed. How sad it is to see hardened hearts and the inability to feel His love, for they cannot receive His love. Their time is running short, for time that isn't computable into eternity isn't enough. Even Jesus's time elapsed in this world; surely ours will too. It isn't eternal on earth because the wages of sin are death. Yes, Jesus lived without sin, but He took ours so we may have eternal life. He ensured our second birth, which is required for us be accounted for in the Book of Life.

Open our eyes, Lord, to Your plan in our lives and Your time for each move we make. Thank You for accepting the cross so we don't need to experience separation from You for all eternity.

But Christ is faithful over God's house as a Son. And we are His house if needed we hold fast our confidence and our boasting in our hope.

(Heb. 3:6 ESV)

DAY 50

Confidence

The Father established confidence in His chosen when He enabled us to possess the Holy Spirit. God is within us; He is our teacher and guide to an eternal picture worthy only by the sacrifice of Jesus. His plan, well executed by the cross, separated the veil that kept us from a personal relationship needed to obtain the Spirit. Now that we have Him within us, we must live our lives in a manner pleasing to the Father. Through consistent meditation on the word of God, our provider gifted us with the interpreter we needed to understand His level of depth. The men chosen to write the Bible were enabled by the Holy Spirit, and the Spirit shows us the design with which they were gifted. "In Hope of eternal life, which God, who never lies, promised before the ages began" (Titus 1:2 ESV).

We so often worry about our next few hours, but the confidence given in the Lord by the Holy Spirit tells us the end. No one can obtain the power to remove Him from our hearts. So, knowing this, why worry about anything? The Spirit is our gift from the Lord Jesus to provide the essentials needed for our spiritual birth in Christ. Before, we had only an earthly commitment, but after spiritual rebirth, we have a godly purpose. The strength we obtain through the Holy Spirit is limitless and so robust we are enriched in its understanding. Through daily effort in God, He shows us more and more through the Spirit. What confidence we have knowing our Creator gives us information through the Spirit. What earthly king gives individual answers and time to each member of his kingdom? Our God gives us an abundance of truth when we seek Him.

Would you buy a car only to walk everywhere you go? Then why do we so often forget the ultimate gift given to man? It took death to break barriers, and it will take spiritual death to obtain new life. "We now have this light shining in our hearts, but we ourselves are like fragile clay jars containing this great treasure. For God, who said, 'Let light shine out of darkness, has shone in our hearts to give the light of the knowledge of the glory of God in the face of Jesus Christ'" (2 Cor. ESV).

Don't ignore what amazing gift God has presented to us at the right time in our lives. He moved at an exact time, but after the emotions settle, we sometimes fall back into our old habits. It would have been better not to have accepted His gift if we will never act on what He is providing for us. We must work to complete holiness that cannot be gifted, for if it was gifted, what reward would it be? Effort for Him gives us our confidence to know we are saved. There are two parts to our walk, Jesus's sacrifice and our longing for the Creator. Good deeds won't get us to where we need to be, but the relationship with our Father, our sacrifices in His name, and our true love for Him will take us to Him.

But one thing is necessary. Mary has chosen the good portion, which will not be taken away from her.

(Luke 10:42 ESV)

DAY 51

Intellect

Our Father's intellect in us is only through the Holy Spirit so an earthly mind can comprehend a heavenly thought. Do we ever ask ourselves, am I truly in it for Him? Now you might be thinking, *Of course, I am.* But truly sit back and think about it. Think about the fears discussed after death has presented itself to us. What comes to mind? Heaven or hell? Does His grace and warmth fill the soul because we know it is Him we seek? Take thoughts of hell out of the equation of life, and what is it that drives us? Our goals or even our families or Him?

Life is a beautiful thing He has gifted each of us with. When you sit back and think about the probability of birth and the statistics of life in this world, our presence alone is a great miracle. Why did He choose us over the other potential people who could have been born to our parents? Our minds must be focused on Him daily, but we cannot chase Him to avoid hell. He knows all our thoughts, genuine or not. If we live the day-to-day life and attend church functions just to go through the numbers, we cannot and won't experience Him. We must live for Him and cherish His presence daily.

John the Baptist was full of the Lord, yet he didn't have a church. John lived in the wilderness, but He and the Father had an irreplaceable relationship. This was because John lived for Him and couldn't have cared less about anything else. Nothing was more important to John. Seek Him first, and you will find His presence; seek the right church, atmosphere, and time, and you will find disappointment. The reason is, He is the only perfect thing in our lives. The ruler of this world is Satan, so nothing can be perfect when death governs the earth.

So why do we fail to see how we trade earthly pleasures for heavenly perfection? Let me be the first to tell you; following Him will be hard and painful at times. We will have our Job moments, but this is due to Satan's governance on earth. We will never know perfection until we pass through heaven's gates. "In that day you will know that I am in my Father, and you in Me, and I in you. Whoever has My commandments and keeps them, he it is who loves Me. And he who loves Me will be loved by My Father, and I will love him and manifest to him" (John 14:20–21 ESV). There aren't enough good deeds you can possibly do to outrun hell. Only the Father's love and your love for Him can rescue you.

Making known to us the mystery of His will, according to His purpose, which He set forth in Christ as a plan for the fullness of time, to unite all things in Him, things in heaven and things on earth.

(Eph. 1:9 ESV)

"I looked at God, and He looked at me, and we were one forever."

—Charles Spurgeon

DAY 52

Purpose

"And proclaim as you go, saying, The Kingdom of Heaven is at hand. Heal the sick, raise the dead, cleanse lepers, cast out demons. You received without paying; give without pay" (Matt. 10:7–8 ESV). "Surely He has borne our griefs and carried our sorrows: Yet we esteem Him stricken, smitten by God and afflicted" (Isaiah 53:4). Jesus healed many with constraints of a man through a heavenly Father. He was God, but on earth, He was limited as man. We so often forget what He charged us with before His death. Heal the sick and raise the dead. Oh, how we tend to overlook things through earthly limitations. Is this due to lack of commitment when we accepted Him and His gift of the Holy Spirit? We have the same Father and conditions Jesus did when He fulfilled His ministry.

How many of us accept Him but never truly change? Do we live for the world or Him? How many churches believe in healing but their pastors are condemned or portrayed as false prophets? Do we even read our Bibles? Sometimes a question needs to be repeated. Jesus asked Peter, "Do you love me?" three times. You are charged to heal, preach, teach, and speak in heavenly tongues. Were these tasks possible only in the times of Christ? No, it starts with failure of purpose and our inability to change. We chose Him by our own free will, and on that day He gave us genuine purpose.

Whether you know it or not, there is a reason you exist. His purpose is your charge, and how we miss this when we fail the simplest task. Live the commandments and know the Word, our Savior. We are so busy setting our own goals that we cannot and won't devote time to prayer and His word. Heaven forbid that He not answer our prayers, though.

"Why, Lord, don't You answer me in my time of need?"

"Because You couldn't spend a moment with Me in peace."

What if that was His answer? Our relationship with the Father is meaningful, and He provides our purpose. He could have chosen anyone else, but He chose us. We need to be prayer warriors and know His word to defend the wars of principalities and evil in this world as well as in unforeseen places. How can we expect anything when we give nothing? All He asks of us is to have a personal relationship with Him and desire Him. When we are able to prove this, He will do the rest almost seamlessly in our lives. This is the simplest of all His tests. When you develop in His word and know His truth, He will share His light. If we commit nothing to our decision in Him, we cannot expect to complete His purpose and see His promises for us. We must unravel His purpose for each of us so we can start completing His miracles for the kingdom.

For you will be a witness for Him to everyone of what you have seen and heard.

(Acts 22:15 ESV)

DAY 53

Gospel

"No one can come to Me unless the Father who sent Me draws him. And I will raise him up on the last day" (John 6:44 ESV). As facilitators of Christ, we can arrange only the initial meeting between the lost and the Father. He will give us the words to communicate to the hearts of people He Himself is already talking to. Christ, being the beginning and the end, came to put a finish to our sins, for He died as a sign of compassion for each of us who chooses Him. He became the crimes we committed against the kingdom as He died on the cross, crimes that deserved our punishment but were taken on His body so He could bear them for us. "For if while we were enemies we were reconciled to God by the death of His Son, much more, now that we were reconciled, shall we be saved by His life" (Rom. 5:10 ESV).

Christ died for us in the past, present, and future. He has the ability to look forward and see who we will become in His name and how we will carry out His purpose in our lives. We have been charged with healing, casting out demons, and teaching the gospel. But is it because we aren't fully devoted to our sanctification that we haven't received the full and mighty power of the Spirit? Is it just the few little imperfections God has told us to be finished with that stand between us and His mighty grace?

"The grace of the Lord Jesus be with all. Amen" (Rev. 22:21 ESV). Removing our sinful ways is not only a life achievement; it is a gift to our Creator. Such a statement is proof we are moving into our holy ways, becoming closer to completing our sanctification, striving to live as Christ did, and fighting the fight for our eternity, which we cannot earn unless our hearts beat His name.

He is coming soon, and we will either fear His return or embrace it with open arms. It would have been better to have never existed than to have never chosen Him of our own free will. What dread it would be to bow before the One we never excepted. Our gospel for the world to see is our natural care for others beyond our care for ourselves, to live for the One whose creation speaks the magnitude of His will and power. Jesus died for us so we may experience His Father. How lucky we are to experience His great gospel and witness it to the world.

I press on toward the goal for the prize of the upward call of God in Christ Jesus. Let those of us who are mature think this way, and if in anything you think otherwise, God will reveal that also to you. Only let us hold true to what we have attained.

(Phil. 3:14–16 ESV)

DAY 54

Maturity

"She listens to no voice: she accepts no correction. She does not trust in the Lord; she does not draw near to her God" (Zeph. 3:2 ESV). Our maturity in our Father starts with trust. His humble necessities provided to us without compromise during our times of weaker seasons are the new growth that enables our maturity. Our unwavering ability to stay focused on Him during life's struggles is strength earned through experience. Time here on earth may be full of trials, but these seasons of development He gifted to us ensure we are prepared for longevity. The heavenly Father produces great fruit not only from blessings but largely from sacrifice. In our sacrifice He expounds on His glory and potential within us.

Since the creation of the earth, there has been only one constant: He reigns among us, within us, and all around us. Every morning we see His art, and as the evening crests, we see His beautiful closure, a completion of consistency but also a taste of His originality. We so often overlook His majesty in the little moments of our busy lives. Daily He tells us to look at the sky and wait in excitement for His return to bring us out of an uncertain world to a place of truth. "For at that time I will change the speech of the peoples to a pure speech, that all of them may call upon the name of the Lord and serve Him with one accord" (Zeph. 3:9

ESV). Our rebellion will no longer last as we are complete and given a new name among the chosen.

Spiritual maturity is a design that cannot be taught; it is lived through obeying our Father's laws and being devoted to keep our focus on Him. As we reach the point that He is the center of our lives, He will show His purpose in us. What an awesome responsibility this is! Rejoice in this because He has entrusted us with an amazing gift. Before we had a name, He assigned our responsibility, which was made true at the cross, and empowered to each of us after our decision to follow His word. Once we have shown how that we have navigated temptation and cast down Satan's trickery, we have proved that we will complete His task without faltering. True love gave His life so we could be gifted with a friendship with the Creator. This cannot be taken lightly because the Creator has now given His plan for us. Our maturity is a key measure in His blueprint for each of our ministries for His kingdom. We must see it is all about Him; it always has been. He created us for friendship, He sent His Son to break the barriers, and He will bring us home for celebration. He is a Father of the prodigal son's and the Lamb.

When the righteous increase, the people rejoice,
but when the wicked rule, the people groan.

(Prov. 29:2 ESV)

When the Spirit of truth comes, He will guide
you into all the truth, for He will not speak on
His own authority, but whatever He hears He
will speak, and He will declare to you the things
that are to come.

(John 16:13 ESV)

DAY 55

Authority

"I will punish the world for its evil, and the wicked for their iniquity; I will put an end to the pomp of the arrogant, and lay low the pompous pride of the ruthless" (Isa. 13:11 ESV). How many times do we forget that our Lord and Savior can end the earth and all its creatures, who are reliant on breath? Let us not take His kindness or silence for weakness, but remember the stories we have been gifted through the Bible. Our Lord destroyed this earth, and although He promised never to destroy it again by flooding, He is coming for His chosen, and every day down is another day closer to redemption. I have to ask, Would we have been better off if the church wasn't reliant on a structure? What if preaching took place in an open area just as Jesus did? We cannot contain the Creator in a box or a church, but we have been gifted with the authority to go forth and create ministries all over the earth.

Jesus told His disciples, "Go forth and make disciples of all nations" under all the authority of heaven. We narrow our own path through limitations of the mind and fear that keep us from doing so through such authority Jesus gave us. We cannot blame Satan for the fears we create for ourselves, those that keep us from God's gracious authority. What we can blame Satan for is compounding our own fears into devastation. That is why we cannot move for Jesus and do not see miracles happening. How do we look to a world of people who want nothing more than to prove our God doesn't exist? When we do nothing outside the church, why is the word *hypocrite* commonly used to describe us? Is it because we exercise our right to worship but fail to exercise our authority to live for Him?

You are the only representation of the Father many will ever see. God's authority given to us is as important as our next breath. Treat everyone you meet as if he or she were Jesus in disguise. How terrible would it be if Jesus walked on earth today and asked for a helping hand or spare change but was judged or treated poorly by a Christian? I couldn't begin to imagine having to answer for that on the day of judgment. "Whoever gives to the poor will not want, but who hides his eyes will get many a curse" (Prov. 28:27 ESV). Many churches are doing unbelievable and amazing things for the kingdom of God. Some are setting an example outside the will of God, and we as the body of Christ need to pull them into the flock. Show them love and mercy; show them the Father. Understanding an honest pagan will keep a good Christian on his or her toes. Walk a life that represents the Father well and shows everyone that our God is merciful and just. Most of all, He is love.

If we say we have fellowship with Him while we walk in darkness, we lie and do not practice the truth. But if we walk in the light, as He is in the light, we have fellowship with one another, and the blood of Jesus His Son cleanses us of all sin.

(1 John 1:6-7 ESV)

DAY 56

Limits

"And you were dead in the trespasses and sins in which you once walked, following the course of this world, following the prince of air, the spirit that is at work in the sons of disobedience" (Eph. 2:1-2 ESV). Limits within our own ministries bind the heavenly potential we could claim from our Father. We at times are the same as the kiss of Judas. We accept Him and His word but turn our backs to the potential ministries in our own lives with the very thing that brought us to Him in the first place. Accepting Him is amazing, but failing to become new is the betrayal of a friend.

The death of Jesus gave us an amazing gift, the gift of friendship. God longs for our companionship, and we owe Him our fellowship. As a thief of the treasury, Judas reopened the door to Satan, and the prince of the air used it to destroy a relationship. Such a simple sin laid the foundation for Judas to sell out his friend for the restitution price of a slave. Something so minuscule was a key moment in the death of Jesus, the exact reason Jesus had to go forth and defeat the grave for us.

In this world, there are and will be many distractions, but do not sell your eternity for such a cheap price. The only fulfillment on this earth is and will always be the Father. For us to think there is any other would be foolish. Our God created the world to spend His time with creation. When we are separated from Him through sin, a void is placed in our hearts, and the only way to fill this emptiness is through Him. That void cannot be filled with anything of this world, because it in itself isn't of this world. "For by the grace you have been saved through faith. And this is not your own doing; it is the gift of God, not as a result of works, so that no one may boast" (Eph. 2:8-9 ESV).

Do not limit the potential for your life God has chosen for you because of sin. Take off the old and put on the new, and unlock God's potential in you. Through trials and hardships, you will show Him you are ready to bear the cup of your ministry, and through faith you will complete it. Our only limits in life are the ones we believe stop us from fulfilling our purpose; most of them are the ones we place on ourselves to keep us safe from risk.

Remember, then, what you received and heard. Keep it, and repent. If you will not wake up, I will come like a thief, and you will not know at what hour I will come against you.

(Rev. 3:3 ESV)

DAY 57

Harvest

"Already the one who reaps is receiving wages and gathering fruit for eternal life, so that sower and reaper may rejoice together" (John 4:36 ESV).

Your harvest is plentiful yet not quite ripe; teach
us how to grow the fields for harvest.
Show us the ones You have chosen at birth,
the ones we are meant to bring to You.
Entrust us with Your words and make
every time we meet momentous.
Show the world Your chosen few are not the
hypocrites they are made to be.
Give us wisdom of heaven to combat the evils
of the world; entrust us with mercy.
Everyone who drinks from Your cup will be
plentiful; those who do not will be lonesome.
Those who cherish the world will have just that;
those who cherish You will have eternity.
Let us long for You; rejoice in understanding
for we are heaven's armies.
What strength You give us to overcome mighty
limits, yet the blind discredits Your power.
Every soul on earth is accountable to You; guide
our light to the ones You gift to us.

Embrace us with Your healing so that
we may bring rest to the lost.
Thank You for taking up a home within our
hearts, such unimaginable grace.
Show us daily our walk so that many will know Your presence.
Victory in Your knowledge for His sacrifice
was the true measure of love.
Rejoice that Your measure of mercy isn't like that of our minds.
Flood the earth with Your water so that
we can embrace the storm of life.
Daily we incur evil; showing the prince of
death our sins won't hold us down.
The time is coming soon for Your harvest;
deliver us from Your winepress of wrath.

Since therefore Christ suffered in the flesh, arm yourselves with the same way of thinking, for whoever has suffered in the flesh has ceased from sin, so as to live for the rest of the time in the flesh no longer for human passions but for the will of God. For the time that is past suffices for doing what the gentiles want to do, living in sensuality, passions, drunkenness, orgies, drinking parties, and lawless idolatry. With respect to this they are surprised when you do not join them in the same flood of debauchery, and they malign you; but they will give an account to Him who is ready to judge the living and the dead.

(1 Peter 4:1–5 ESV)

DAY 58

Grace

"Above all, keep loving one another earnestly, since love covers a multitude of sins. Show hospitality to one another without grumbling. As each has received a gift, use it to serve one another, as good stewards of God's varied grace" (1 Peter 4:8–10 ESV). What good would come if the Christian pointed out the nonbeliever's faults? What would Christ gain from our self-righteousness? What power would the Creator entrust to us if this is how we treat His lost sheep? He would leave the ninety nine walking with Him to find the one that was lost and disobedient. Remember, we were all born into sin, and sin is death. "There is only one lawgiver and judge, he who is able to save and to destroy. But who are you to judge your neighbor?" (James 4:12 ESV).

Our judge gave His only Son to redeem all of us from sin; do we understand the significance? The bar has been wiped clean for us who have accepted Him, so why do we receive such a gift to stain it with judgment? For if we were once not of perfect cloth, why should we remind those who are not? Showing God's grace enables the movement of Christ in one's soul. It is a gift to show people Jesus, and it confirms that God's gift of love resides in our hearts. Remain steadfast; the ones of Christ like glory. The mercy of the King is represented in you, and either the world will know Him or distrust Him because of the depiction of your actions. You have been entrusted with the grace of a Creator who has shown you grace by forgetting your past and looking to your future for blessed fruits. Christ was the perfect sacrifice. "Since it is written, 'You shall be Holy, for I am Holy'" (1 Peter 1:16 ESV). Sanctification means to give up all at the cross of Jesus and move toward God's love; it can be achieved only once we surrender all.

> In their case the god of this world has blinded the minds of the unbelievers, to keep them from seeing the light of the gospel of the glory of Christ, who is the image of God.

(2 Cor. 4:4 ESV)

DAY 59

Miracles

This age is much like the ages of the past; the ruler of death forms a hard spirit within many. Given situations and circumstances, we have the ability to show people Jesus; no matter the outcome, He is present through us. Our faith, love, and mercy are maybe the only Jesus some may experience. We don't need to force Him on anyone, just allow His presence in any given situation. He is the almighty Creator. He can handle the problem at hand, but if you do not show Jesus in the little moments of life, why would He choose to make His presence known through you? It's all about being a facilitator for God and His works.

Christ spoke what the Father told Him; He acted when the Father moved. He healed whom the Father instructed Him to heal. When we recognize that no matter how bad you want to make a difference in another's life, He must instruct your actions and set the stage for the Spirit. We must do things and carry out His gospel on earth as Jesus did, but we have to serve Him and trust Him during the process. We have to ask for His guidance in our actions and interactions so we understand how He wants us to carry out His movements.

When we lay it all down for Him and give Him all our trust, we can move mountains in His name. Miracles are more common than we may realize. If winning the lottery is about 1 out of 175 million, then that in itself would be a miracle if you won. But using that same example, the fact that you were born out of the other possible candidates to your parents is about 1 out of 250 million. We tend to forget that our Creator has a specific purpose for each of us, and if we never asked, we may never understand the very question that keeps people up at night. Why do I exist, and what am I going to do in this life?

Sometimes we have to look to see the daily miracles He provides for us. The difference is when we come like a child; we see things as He wants us to. When we see things as He wishes, then we can act on them as He wants; thus, another miracle comes from our obedience. "Now the Lord is the Spirit, and where the Spirit of the Lord is, there is freedom. And we all, with unveiled face, beholding the glory of the Lord, are being transformed into the same image from one degree of glory to another. For this comes from the Lord who is the Spirit" (2 Cor. 3:17–18 ESV). Christ removes the veil that keeps us from seeing God; through faith we are resurrected in Christ to move into good standing with our Father. He removes the stone and fashions the path to our Creator.

I can do nothing on My own. As I hear, I judge,
and My judgement is just, because I seek not My
own will but the will of Him who sent Me.

(John 5:30 ESV)

DAY 60

Obedience

As Jesus was obedient to God, His Father, we should be also, listening for His guidance in every step of our daily lives. We should be subservient to His message, just as the manna of life was laid in front of us to guide our path to His purpose. He will always provide what we need, even if it is an obstacle to teach us how to entrust Him with our lives. Even in our struggles, we should ask, What am I to learn from this, Lord? What strength are You preparing me for? What am I to do now? How do I get through this? I need Your guidance so I can make the sound decision; not my will be done but Yours. He will provide us with bread and seed to be sowed to advance His works in this world for the kingdom. The bread is ours to revitalize us in mind and body to keep us focused and prepared for when He moves in our lives. "Do not work for the food that perishes, but for the food that endures to eternal life, which the Son of Man will give to you. For on Him the Father has set His seal" (John 6:27 ESV).

Jesus is the Bread of Life; no other can give us the heavenly substance we need to endure the journey we have in God. He keeps us nourished in what the Father has taught Him and passed through us from the Spirit to continue His works in this world. It isn't intended to conduct these works to purchase our ticket to heaven but to facilitate others and assist them in their journey to the kingdom. We cannot purchase our way to Him; Jesus already did that for each of us. There are many who are lost and don't understand their price for heaven was paid at the cross. We are to show them so their light will shine on a world as dark as ours. "It is the Spirit who gives life; the flesh is no help at all. The words that I have spoken to you are Spirit and Life" (John 6:63 ESV).

Jesus knew who would betray Him from the beginning, not just the son of deception. Is it betrayal if we have known Him and ignored His purpose in us? Jesus was entirely obedient to our Father; why at times do we fail in this obedience? What break, though, in our lives did we miss in our disobedience? "For my flesh is true food, and my blood is true drink. Whoever feeds on my flesh and drinks my blood abides in me, and I in Him. As the living Father sent Me, and I live because of the Father, so whoever feeds on Me, he also will live because of Me. This is the bread that came down from Heaven, not like the bread the fathers ate, and died. Whoever feeds on this bread will live forever" (John 6:55–58 ESV).

May we listen to Your words with open ears; let our hearts feel Your presence overwhelmingly and our eyes see Your truth daily. Amen

In the beginning, God created the Heavens and the earth. The earth was without form and void, and darkness was over the face of the deep. And the Spirit of God was hovering over the face of the waters.

(Gen. 1:1–2 ESV)